Praise for *Reengineering Health Care*

"*Reengineering Health Care* gets to the core of transforming our current system by advocating the widespread use of IT, eliminating inefficient practices, and keeping the system focused on a healthy individual and not on a broken process."

—*Newt Gingrich, Founder of the Center for Health Transformation, and former Speaker of the U.S. House of Representatives*

"Processes in health care organizations are filled with workarounds, redundancy, and work that does not add value. This book is a prescription for streamlining health care. Using the same techniques that have successfully transformed business into customer-focused, nimble, and efficient organizations, the authors provide a step-by-step approach to improving health care processes. Champy and Greenspun are uniquely qualified to guide health care into the next generation of Lean delivery systems."

—*Dr. John Halamka, Chief Information Officer, Beth Israel Deaconess Medical Center*

"In health care, we tend to inundate our people with information, rather than enabling them to have insights. This concise guide will resonate with both senior and front-line managers who know they're engaged in unproductive work. They will see that reengineering is not overly difficult and can enable them to improve patient care and efficiency."

—*Trevor Fetter, President and CEO, Tenet Health Corporation, and Trustee, Federation of American Hospitals*

"It isn't reform that will fix our ailing health care system, its reengineering. Champy and Greenspun (engineer and clinician) reference organizations large and small that have transformed and sometimes reinvented themselves by reengineering care delivery. In so doing they've lowered costs, improved care quality and patient safety, and increased the satisfaction of those giving and receiving care. These organizations have been successful by incorporating best practices from other industries, respecting the sanctity of people over technology, and using engineering discipline to plan and implement improvements to their programs and services. Every clinician, clinic administrator, hospital executive, and politician should read this book."

—Bill Crounse, M.D., *Senior Director, Worldwide Health, Microsoft Corporation*

"Implement health care technology, and you have better health care tools; reengineer with a focus on technology, process, and people, and you have a better health care system. Champy and Greenspun have produced a straightforward guide on how to transform health care with the resulting opportunity to maximize quality, safety, convenience, and positively impact the cost of delivery. Using case studies, the authors show not only how much more can be realized when we change process and culture as well as technology, but also how critical the need is for reengineering. No one can read this book and not feel a profound call to action."

—H. Stephen Lieber, *CAE, President & CEO, HIMSS*

REENGINEERING HEALTH CARE

A Manifesto for Radically Rethinking Health Care Delivery

JIM CHAMPY
HARRY GREENSPUN, M.D.

Printed in the United States of America

First Printing June 2010

ISBN-10: 0-13-705265-0
ISBN-13: 978-0-13-705265-3

Pearson Education LTD.
Pearson Education Australia PTY, Limited.
Pearson Education Singapore, Pte. Ltd.
Pearson Education North Asia, Ltd.
Pearson Education Canada, Ltd.
Pearson Educatión de Mexico, S.A. de C.V.
Pearson Education—Japan
Pearson Education Malaysia, Pte. Ltd.

Library of Congress Cataloging-in-Publication Data is on file

Vice President, Publisher
Tim Moore

Associate Publisher and Director of Marketing
Amy Neidlinger

Editorial Assistant
Pamela Boland

Operations Manager
Gina Kanouse

Senior Marketing Manager
Julie Phifer

Publicity Manager
Laura Czaja

Assistant Marketing Manager
Megan Colvin

Cover Designer
Gary Adair

Managing Editor
Kristy Hart

Senior Project Editor
Lori Lyons

Proofreader
Language Logistics, Inc.

Indexer
Cheryl Lenser

Compositor
Nonie Ratcliff

Manufacturing Buyer
Dan Uhrig

For my wife, Lois, from whom
I have learned so much;
for my son, Adam, who has now
become my teacher;
and for all those who provide
care to our family.

—JAC

For my family for their support,
my colleagues for their teaching,
and my patients for their inspiration.

—HGG

CONTENTS

ACKNOWLEDGMENTS

A book of this kind is only written with the collaboration of others. We are grateful to all who have helped and challenged us along the way. Our thanks go to the talented editors and researchers at Wordworks, Inc.: Donna Sammons Carpenter, Maurice Coyle, Ruth Hlavacek, Molly Jones, Larry Martz, Cindy Butler Sammons, and Robert Stock. We also thank Helen Rees and Joan Mazmanian of the Helen Rees Literary Agency for their sound advice and counsel, and Barbara Hendra and Danny Stern for their publishing wisdom.

We are deeply appreciative of the efforts of our publisher, Tim Moore, and all his colleagues at Pearson: Amy Neidlinger, Megan Colvin, Julie Phifer, Gary Adair, Lori Lyons, Nonie Ratcliff, and Cheryl Lenser. And our capable assistants, Dee Dee Haggerty, Judy Bennett, and Trina Wellendorf have once again helped to make us productive.

But we are most grateful to the real heroes of this book, the people who are changing health care and inspiring others to do the same. You will soon hear their names and voices, but we call them out here because this book would not have been possible without their courage, vision, and actions:

Catherine Camenga, RN
Florence Chang
Matt Eisenberg, MD
Debra A. Geihsler
Nan L. Holland, RN
Thomas W. Knight, MD
Scharmaine Lawson Baker, RN
Maggie Lohnes, RN
Zeev E. Neuwirth, MD
Cheryl Pegus, MD

Finally, as always, we are grateful to our famlies who support us in our work and whose care and wellbeing further inspire us to write this book.

ABOUT THE AUTHORS

Jim Champy is one of the leading management and business thinkers of our time. His first best seller, *Reengineering the Corporation*, remains the bible for executing process change. His second book, *Reengineering Management*, another best seller, was recognized by *Business Week* as one of the most important books of its time. Champy's latest books, *OUTSMART!* and *INSPIRE!*, show how to achieve breakthrough growth and engage customers, in even the toughest marketplace.

Champy is also an experienced manager and advisor. He is the former Chairman of Consulting for Dell Perot Services. He speaks and writes with the authority of real business experience. For years, he has also been an advisor to multiple health care systems, where he has brought his pragmatism to the need for change.

Go to www.jimchampy.com for more about the book and an ongoing dialogue.

Harry Greenspun, M.D., is the Chief Medical Officer of Dell Inc., providing strategic leadership with a clinical perspective. He has held a diverse range of clinical and executive roles across the industry, giving him a unique perspective on the challenges and opportunities faced in health care. In 2010, *Modern Healthcare* magazine named him one of the "50 Most Powerful Physician Executives in Healthcare." Prior to working for Dell, he served as Chief Medical Officer for Northrop Grumman Corporation, providing subject matter expertise and strategic direction in military and veterans' health, life sciences, and public health.

A recognized expert in health policy, Dr. Greenspun has advised the Obama administration and Congress on health care reform. He serves on the World Economic Forum's Global Health Advisory Board, and the boards of numerous universities, health care organizations, and publications.

Dr. Greenspun received his medical degree from the University of Maryland and completed his residency and fellowship at the Johns Hopkins Hospital, where he served as chief resident in the Department of Anesthesiology and Critical Care Medicine. As a cardiac anesthesiologist, he has practiced in major academic medical centers, as well as community hospitals.

INTRODUCTION

Imagine a world in which the delivery of health care is of the highest quality and so efficient that it is affordable to every person—and government. Today, that world seems distant, but not because of lack of progress in the diagnosis and treatment of illness and disease. Science and technology are enabling new cures and techniques at a rate never experienced before. The world we seek is beyond our reach because the work of delivering health care has not kept pace with advances in science and technology.

When you consider that most of us spend half of our waking lives performing something called "work," you'd think we would be really good at it, right?

Well, half right. And the missing half explains why so much of even our most advanced toil is often inefficient and hence ineffective.

Examples abound, but this book focuses on an industry and calling crucial to the well-being of everyone—health care. Inefficient and ineffective health care can take its toll in human lives while also devouring our personal and national wealth and resources.

Inefficient and ineffective health care can take its toll in human lives while also devouring our personal and national wealth and resources.

Not long ago, America's health caregivers began addressing the complex issue of patient records—all the vast, painstakingly recorded details that are supposed to help doctors diagnose and prescribe. With great fanfare, hospitals and physicians slowly began using computers to keep track of those records. Their accomplishment was hailed as the start of a new era of efficiency and safety in health care delivery.

But as I write, a team of Harvard researchers studying 3,000 hospitals across the United States has determined that electronic health recordkeeping has not been widely adopted. And where computerization is being used, it has proven far less beneficial to patient care than expected. In fact, it sometimes complicates and even diminishes care by flooding nurses and physicians with information that takes providers away from their patients while raising privacy concerns that are both real and imagined. Not long ago, I heard the head of nursing at a large hospital take up the subject at a leadership meeting. "We came here to care for patients," she said, "but now we spend more time pushing paper and sitting in front of computer screens."

Computers aren't the problem. Technology can indeed work wonders in improving health care delivery. The problem lies in the application of technology and, more basically, in the way in which the work of health care delivery has been organized.

This crucial issue of how to improve work performance in all kinds of fields has obsessed me for more than two decades. It started in 1988 when my associate, the late Michael Hammer, and I had a life-changing experience: We visited Toyota. We already knew that the Japanese automaker had developed unique methods that dramatically improved operations. But we discovered something more—Toyota was already far more efficient than its U.S. rivals. (This was years before the company's unfortunate quality problems. The recent breakdowns remind us that even high-performing enterprises must remain vigilant in their quest for efficiency and effectiveness. It's a lesson that applies equally to health care, as you will see in the pages ahead.)

We realized that, unlike Toyota, many large companies had allowed their work to become fragmented, overly specialized, and compartmentalized. One insurance company we visited took 24 days to issue a simple policy, a job that required only 10 minutes of actual work! It turned out that this one 10-minute piece of paperwork had to crawl through 17 different departments, most of which added no value whatever to the process.

Mike and I were trained as engineers. We thought work should be an efficient progression of connected tasks that produced a worthwhile product or service. We wanted companies to run like well-tuned engines—no sputtering, coughing, or failing, unlike so many companies we knew of.

We searched for a new way of doing work that would achieve two goals at once—increase a company's efficiency while improving the quality of its products and services. We cast aside the notion of work as a collection of independent tasks. We thought related tasks should be combined as discrete processes, each of which delivered a valuable output. For instance, sales and marketing departments should stop acting separately and, instead, join forces in a larger process called "new customer acquisition." Similarly, everyone with a separate hand in developing products should pool with all other developers in a single process called "new product launch."

Together, Mike and I wrote *Reengineering the Corporation: A Manifesto for Business Revolution.* I am both humbled and proud to say that the book is still in print in more than 20 languages. And I believe the idea of redesigning work is even more important and powerful today. Technological advances, especially the Internet and the proliferation of smart mobile devices, enable enterprises to go even further in work redesign, reaching new levels of efficiency and performance.

REENGINEERING: RX FOR HEALTH CARE DELIVERY

For years, I have pondered why reengineering, has not been widely applied to health care. As an engineer and consultant observing clinicians at work, I see a series of delivery processes waiting to be organized for maximum effectiveness. Each process is typically discrete; it consists of specific activities and has an overall input and output. But these health care processes are hardly arranged in the most effective possible sequences. In fact, they are rife with opportunity for a redesign to maximize their quality, safety, convenience, and cost of delivery.

Yes, we have made amazing progress in the diagnosis and treatment of illness and disease over the past 50 years. But not enough has changed in the processes of delivering health care.

At a meeting of hospital executives not long ago, I listened to a discussion of ways to improve an error rate of 2 percent in giving patients the correct medication. I was alarmed—2 percent, for a pill that might kill? Why not zero errors? I became even more concerned when someone pointed out that the near-miss error rate was closer to 11 percent. What accounted for the 9 percentage-point differential? I asked. The answer: vigilant nurses who recognized—in time—that someone had inadvertently selected the wrong medication for a patient's condition. How could such a thing happen? One of the executives handed me a couple of handwritten orders, scrawled by doctors in a hurry. The cliché about doctors' writing held true. They were unreadable.

Many hospitals already require doctors to enter all prescriptions electronically, but that is only the first step in addressing this broken and potentially deadly task. A single hospital may administer hundreds of thousands of medication dosages each year and, as you will read in the pages to come, each dose administered can involve dozens of steps. The opportunity for error is plain to see, with or without electronic entry. The solution is to rethink and reengineer the work.

THE CULTURE OF HEALTH CARE

You might fairly ask whether reengineering can be applied to health care delivery. After all, the concept has come out of business management, while health care has a culture all its own.

My answer has two parts: First, I firmly believe that reengineering could and should be applied to any kind of work, from factory production to health care, and even the writing of prose. Second, I both recognize and admire the culture of health care, particularly as it's practiced by clinicians. They come to work not only to "do no harm," as Hippocrates prescribed, but to use their knowledge for actually doing good.

I also believe that critics, sometimes physicians themselves, can be harsh in their assessment of how medical practitioners do what they do. "Physicians just don't think that way" was a sentiment we heard more than once in interviewing people for this book.

Well, physicians aren't the only ones who find it difficult to conceive or understand the processes that make up their work. I've met many business executives who were equally flummoxed when it came to understanding the design of work and process. And why should they? It is a matter of training, not of culture. Physicians, like many business managers in the past, have been trained to accomplish what they have to accomplish independently, not in teams. The problem arises because health care delivery today demands teamwork.

But I have no doubt that physicians are capable of changing how they do what they do, as well as their behaviors. I've seen it in many health care settings across the country. As the examples in this book illustrate, it's all about socialization, education, and training.

The high sense of purpose that infuses clinicians' work is, in my estimation, the motivating force for reengineering health care delivery. I am convinced that clinicians will be guided by their larger mission. They will listen carefully, reconsider how they are doing their work now, and thoroughly study any changes that can help them do even more good.

ABOUT HARRY

I knew from the start that I would need expert help in carrying the message of reengineering to hospitals and clinicians. I would need a gifted partner well acquainted with health care delivery and all possible ways this unique kind of work might be redesigned.

I am privileged to have Dr. Harry Greenspun join me as co-author of this book. His background and experience make him the ideal bridge between the world of business and the culture of health care.

After receiving his bachelor's degree from Harvard and his medical degree from the University of Maryland, Harry completed his training and served as Chief Resident at Johns Hopkins. He then practiced as a cardiac anesthesiologist in community hospitals and academic medical centers. He has been an educator and a consultant with special expertise in information technology and health care policy, and has served as chief medical officer for major corporations. Early in his career, he founded a company that tracked clinical outcomes in cardiac surgery.

Harry is now the Chief Medical Officer at Dell Inc. and is an active member of multiple forums working on national health care reform. At Dell, he engages with health care providers—both hospitals and physicians—that are adopting new technologies to improve the delivery of care. Harry brings real experience and expertise to health care reengineering and truly understands the opportunity cost of doing nothing.

Upon meeting other physicians, often men and women with international reputations for excellence, Harry likes to ask how do we know if we are being good doctors? As they ponder this question, Harry's friends recognize that there are few objective measures. The point he's making is that in most parts of this country and around the world, physicians have few valid ways to benchmark their performance against that of their peers or any other clear standard.

Through decades of malpractice litigation, expert witnesses have regularly established when the "standard of care" has been violated. Yet, there are few examples of excellence. Hospitals, large practices, health plans, and medical societies often collect and analyze data for quality improvement, but the results are typically designed to raise providers to some acceptable minimum standard of care or to root out outliers.

When rigorous quality reporting and transparency efforts are established, Harry says, the results are often enlightening, sometimes revealing that a reputedly high-quality organization is, in fact, quite mediocre, an emperor without clothes, so to speak.

As a doctor himself, Harry has always strived to practice good medicine, but his report card was based on what he considered to be weak indicators—referrals to friends and requests from surgeons to assist in particularly challenging cases. But he says he could never be sure whether he was a really gifted anesthesiologist or just an average or lucky one who was easy to work with and had a good bedside manner.

Harry rightly determined that if we accept that doctors are practicing medicine without knowing whether they are actually doing a good job—and we know through the examples highlighted in this book that doctors are capable of performing at a much higher level of safety, efficiency, and effectiveness—a disturbing picture emerges: In our current state, doctors may be practicing not only at a substandard level compared to their peers; they may be practicing at a level far below what their own capabilities enable.

Those individuals and organizations that complain about the hassle, expense, and upheaval caused by launching a reengineering effort should consider the opportunity cost. Is the detriment to your patients, practices, and peers worth the delay? Harry and I would both agree that the answer is a definite "no." And we believe that reengineering presents an opportunity for physicians to practice at a level to which they aspire.

As this book unfolds, you will discover that reengineering health care will require changes both to the work performed and to traditional patterns of behavior. In our desire to gain and hold your attention, Harry and I may raise our voices from time to time. But we do so with the greatest respect for those on the frontlines of health care delivery. You will see examples drawn from organizations large and small, many well known, others less so. We hope our efforts will make a serious contribution to your work.

—*Jim Champy*

CHAPTER 1

WHY REENGINEER HEALTH CARE?

Health care costs too much and achieves too little for one profound reason—it is tremendously inefficient. And because of that inefficiency, quality issues abound.

Some view improving efficiency in health care as simply getting doctors to see more patients each hour. Our view is different. In these pages, we present the stories of ingenious people and organizations, large and small, that have found ways to do the job better. They have reduced tensions and improved communication among medical team members, enormously improving performance. They have reprioritized the physician's day, leaving more time for patients. They have engaged patients along a continuum of care across a fragmented system. And they have made the delivery of care safer.

What these pioneers also have in common is an approach to their work known as reengineering, a term that entered the business lexicon after *Reengineering the Corporation* was published in 1993. It ignited a widespread movement to improve the way work is performed by businesses. In essence, reengineering sees work not as a series of separate tasks to be individually optimized, but as groupings of interconnected processes to be reassessed and reinvented *in toto*.

The book formally defined reengineering as "the fundamental rethinking and radical redesign of business processes to achieve dramatic improvements in critical, contemporary measures of performance, such as cost, quality, service, and speed." Four words—fundamental, radical, dramatic, and process—are the keys to reengineering.

Fundamental refers to how work is performed and the basic questions that need to be asked: Are the underlying assumptions about the design of work still valid? Have advances in science and technology enabled work to be performed in new, more effective ways?

Radical means going beyond superficial changes in the way things are being done. You need to ask whether old structures and operating assumptions are diminishing the quality and service being delivered by your enterprise. Do you need to go back to your original roots to rethink how work should be done?

Dramatic tells you that reengineering isn't about marginal or incremental improvements. Sometimes an enterprise—or an entire industry—requires something more than piecemeal change. Has your organization reached a point where it's survival or efficacy is threatened in a way that only wholesale change can fix?

Finally, process refers to a group of activities that uses one or more kinds of input to create an output a customer values. In health care, the customer might be a patient, a clinician, or the entity paying for the care.

For the past 20 years, enterprises have relied on reengineering, or reengineering-like thinking, to achieve success. Companies as diverse as Texas Instruments, Campbell Soup, and Wal-Mart have successfully reengineered. The methodologies and techniques may vary in name, but they all share the same ambition for dramatic improvement in the performance of work by focusing on process.

Observers of health care agree that a compelling case exists for radical improvement and dramatic change in care delivery. So for the purposes of this book, we suggest a more appropriate definition of reengineering: The radical improvement of health care delivery processes to enhance quality and dramatically lower costs, while also greatly expanding patient accessibility to that improved care.

Implicit in this definition is our belief that more efficient and safer delivery will automatically lead to sharply reduced costs. More to the point, without reengineering, we don't see how any economy will ever be able to afford health care for all of its citizens.

Reengineering must be done, and it must be done by clinicians. No angel of government, even under the auspices of "national health care reform," can reduce the cost and improve the quality of health care without the work and leadership of clinicians. It's time for all clinicians—physicians, nurses, technicians, physician assistants, and pharmacists— to assume their rightful role in directing change.

Reengineering must be done, and it must be done by clinicians. No angel of government, even under the auspices of "national health care reform," can reduce the cost and improve the quality of health care without the work and leadership of clinicians.

By and large, health care has evaded both the rigors and rewards of reengineering. But there is no reason why that state of affairs should continue. Health care is ripe for reengineering, and signs point to adoption of those principles in certain segments of medical practice.

DRAMATIC CHANGE IS POSSIBLE

Meet Geisinger Health System, a 93-year-old network of three hospitals and an insurance company based in Danville, Pennsylvania. Geisinger recruited its CEO, Dr. Glenn Steele, a surgeon and oncologist, from the University of Chicago medical faculty in 2003. Ahead of many health care institutions, Geisinger was open to change, and having its own hospitals and health-insurance plan made it ideal for controlled experiments with a reengineering concept now known as ProvenCare.

The problem at hand was the huge variation in care that comes with dividing patient responsibility among multiple specialists. Since doctors use different protocols and possess different communication skills, patient outcomes were unpredictable. The variations increased relapses, which, in turn, caused more readmissions and drove up patient costs.

Starting with coronary-artery bypass surgery, a common, well-studied procedure with repeatable, refineable processes, Steele and seven cardiothoracic surgeons focused on how to solve the care-variation problem. They first decided to consider the work of a bypass as a process, then they developed a master list of 40 essential steps in patient treatment, ranging from initial visit to discharge. The individual treatment steps were well-known, of course; the new wrinkle was the innovative way in which Steele and his team chose to consider each step as part of a larger process, and to make sure that all steps got done every time.

To make this happen, ProvenCare provides bonuses for doctors who follow the established, written protocol. Those who see good reason to skip a step (very few have) must explain why in the patient's record. The ultimate goal is to confirm that no step has been forgotten, whether applied or not.

Preliminary studies show that ProvenCare's coronary bypass program significantly reduces hospital stays, patient bills, and readmission rates. Geisinger has now applied the approach to other procedures, including hip replacement, cataract surgery, and diabetes management.

But while there's no doubt that meticulous use of well-designed checklists can and does improve health care delivery, that's only one facet of what's needed to reengineer care as a whole. The breakthroughs we cite in the pages ahead, coupled with our analyses and comments, are organized to illustrate the three main pillars of our approach: technology, process, and people. Let's take each in turn.

- ▶ *Technology.* In any science-based enterprise, technological developments offer daily opportunities for redesigning work. Do you automatically consider technological solutions to the problems you find in delivering health care? Are you monitoring new technology for developments that might enhance performance in your hospital or practice? How do you find new technology that will mesh with your total system to work efficiently? Are you doing enough to reduce risks? Are you prepared to install the best available systems for fast, reliable communication among doctors, nurses, and administrators—and to make sure that they fit with the redesigned work of your organization? How far along are you in developing electronic health care records?

- ▶ *Process.* Whether or not new technology is applied, an organization's work is best understood as a collection of processes. What's the best technique for determining which processes need improvement? Once identified, how do you develop a strategy for getting the results you desire? How should work be reordered? Which frontline employees—nurses, administrative staff, doctors—should play what roles? How and to whom should changes be introduced, and should they be carried out sequentially or simultaneously?

▶ *People*. No process can work properly without people trained as a team to execute. Are existing relationships within your organization helpful or harmful to high performance? What programs are needed to prepare doctors and nurses for change? Are you open to listening to your people's criticisms of new methods and to support innovations designed to adapt to the real world? How do you develop leaders in hospitals or practices who will accept, strengthen, and maintain new standards?

Of course, people, process, and technology do not exist in isolation. The interfaces among them can either enhance or detract from the overall performance of an organization and the ultimate outcome and experience of the patient.

But before we begin detailed descriptions of pioneering programs focused on technology, processes, and people, let's meet a health care reformer whose reengineering achievements integrate all three approaches. Chapter 2 tells the story of Zeev Neuwirth, one of this country's most persistent and productive innovators in health care delivery.

CHAPTER 2

MEET ZEEV NEUWIRTH, REENGINEER

Zeev Neuwirth had no notion of curing the health care delivery system when he first got into medicine. He trained at the University of Pennsylvania School of Medicine and completed his internship and residency in internal medicine at Mount Sinai Medical Center in New York City. Near the end of his residency, in 1989, Neuwirth decided to add a subspecialty in cardiology. But with student loans accumulating, he put his fellowship on hold and took a job as an attending physician at the Veterans Administration Hospital in the Bronx. There, his professional path took a critical turn when he became fascinated with the way physicians treated patients—not so much as medical cases, but how they treated them as people. It was the start of a journey that led him to abandon his pursuit of cardiology and begin investigating health care delivery in hospitals and physicians' offices.

Assigned to manage the ambulatory care department, Neuwirth was distressed to see that people were talking past each other. The medical personnel weren't listening to the patients and their families, and the patients saw the doctors as rude, arrogant, and lacking empathy. Meanwhile, the physicians felt misunderstood and disrespected by the administration, and the entire medical staff thought no one was listening to them.

A separate and huge issue for physicians was the
constant worry over being sued by patients who
smoked, ate all the wrong foods, never exercised,
didn't take their medications or show up for
appointments but still expected medical miracles. All
in all, the doctors, nurses, and staff were exhausted,
overwhelmed, and quite jaded.

Neuwirth began to focus on communication
between doctors and patients, looking outside the
medical literature for solutions and giving seminars
to the medical community. His work drew national
attention, and in 1993, *Forbes* magazine wrote about
the changes being made within the VA system. A
couple of years later, Neuwirth was part of a team
that used the VA platform to launch the first national
program to improve doctor-patient communication.

Then, in the latter part of the decade, Neuwirth's
perspective changed. His seminars had led him to
conclude that poor communication was just one
aspect of a much bigger problem. "I realized that the
doctor and patient weren't the only people involved
in health care delivery," he told us. "I had been
trained to believe that the doctor delivered medicine
and everyone else was a bit player."

"But as I observed clinical interactions, I saw that
view was wrong. There was a whole system that

included nurses, physician assistants, medical assistants, secretaries, technicians, receptionists, administrators—and, of course, the patient and his or her family. And patient care—the patient's whole experience, from the standpoint of quality, safety, respectful and dignified treatment—all of it depended on a system that worked well. But the system was badly broken." And before the system could be repaired, he concluded, it had to be understood.

To gain that understanding, Neuwirth embarked on an odyssey that illuminates what's wrong with the system while also providing strong examples of promising repairs.

His solutions make use of technology, but they are mostly centered on the process and people pillars of the reengineering equation. Technology is "just not my thing," he told us. "I have nothing against technology, but I don't lead with it.

"My definition of innovation centers around understanding needs—the needs of patients, their families, and health care providers—and creating practical, patient-oriented, more effective solutions that are less costly and easier for people to use. And whether or not you use technology to get there is really not the point. What we need is a continuum of care, a coordinated and integrated process that listens to both the patient and the provider. Instead, what we often get is technology embedded in the same old paradigm of piecemeal medicine."

Born in Israel and raised in New Jersey, Neuwirth graduated from Tufts University with Phi Beta Kappa and summa cum laude distinction in 1983. He decided to become a physician—not for prestige or money, but so he could spend his days interacting with people and applying science. He says he sailed through medical training at Penn and Mt. Sinai "without really experiencing life," an omission quickly corrected when he found himself in charge of primary care at the Bronx VA hospital. Once he began taking a systems view of health care, he enrolled at Manhattan's renowned Ackerman Institute for the Family, where he spent four years of nights and weekends studying team building and human systems. After leaving Ackerman, Neuwirth trained in group therapy with a focus on leadership and community organizing.

Moving on from the Bronx and the VA, Neuwirth joined Lenox Hill Hospital on Manhattan's Upper East Side as part of its full-time Internal Medicine residency training faculty. He soon began working with teams of physician residents to change their interactions with patients. The emergency room, in particular, had poor patient satisfaction scores, falling somewhere in the lowest third of ERs nationwide. Neuwirth used his group therapy skills to help change the ER culture.

"You didn't need a patient-satisfaction survey to tell you that the ER was in trouble," he told us. "You could feel the tension," and it wasn't really about patient care but, rather, the way the staff interacted among themselves and with outsiders. "There were factions and infighting and backstabbing," Neuwirth said, in a cold and actively hostile environment that extended to other departments in the hospital. "With no one talking to anyone else, it wasn't a great leap to understand how errors could be creeping in. The lack of trust and respect was clearly affecting patient care."

Although the chief of internal medicine had sent Neuwirth down to see what he could do to fix things in the ER, the ER director was not particularly accommodating. "You can't take people off their jobs," he told Neuwirth when he suggested doing some team-building work, "they're needed in the ER. And when they're not working, you can't ask them to come in before or after their shifts, either."

Finally, Neuwirth got the director to agree to let him talk to one person for one hour. "Give me your bad player," he said, which happened to be a clinician who also had an administrative role. Neuwirth met with the man the next day in a quiet, unfurnished back room of the ER. "I started by telling him that I wasn't sent by human resources and this had nothing to do with him personally. 'We're trying to clear up some issues in the ER,' I said, 'and I decided to start with you because you play a key role here and, from what I've been told by your director, you're having some difficulties.'"

From his psychological training, Neuwirth knew that the person singled out—in this case, the "bad player"—is often just the one manifesting a widespread problem. And in any system, the issues are typically not about the individual but about the underlying processes and structures in place.

"I got him talking about himself," Neuwirth told us, "where he came from, his disadvantaged background, how he put himself through school and became a physician's assistant. He was very proud of what he had accomplished and the work he was doing now. He struck me as a very genuine person with good values and good intentions who was frustrated by administrative roadblocks in the ER. I let him know that I was trying to help the ER and had long shared his frustration with bureaucracies."

Having formed something of a bond with the clinician, Neuwirth asked him to describe what was going well in the ER. "That's a family therapy technique," he explained, "an exception-to-the-rule approach that shifts the focus away from the negative and opens a path to aspirational thinking and positive change." At that point, the clinician began to describe a situation in which everyone in the ER performed perfectly when a patient with chest pain came in.

The clinician had taken the call ahead of time and immediately had a cardiology team ready to assist when the patient arrived. The handoff was brilliant, he said, with nurses, doctors, physicians' assistants, and all the appropriate equipment in place and operating as expected. The IV was inserted, the EKG monitor turned on, the cardiologist made a diagnosis and ordered the correct medication, the operating room was notified, the surgical team was suiting up—the clinician described it as "being in the zone. Everything was just flowing; people didn't even have to talk. And that's the way we should be all the time," he told Neuwirth.

"Listening to him speak was almost like watching a movie where you go from the bad beginning to the part where you begin to hear the music swell," Neuwirth said. "And I told the clinician that I was 'feeling good about this ER after hearing that story, and I think there's got to be a way to make this kind of experience happen more often.' He said, 'Yeah, now that we're talking about it, I'm sure there is.' I suggested he talk to his director about what could be done to make things better.

"But the first thing I want you to do, I told him, is pass this forward. My hour is up, but you can pick someone else in the ER and bring that person to this same room and do what we just did: Ask about the person's background and how they came to the ER, spend a few minutes listening to their complaints, and then ask about a time when things worked really well for a patient. Do it just as we did, get a blow-by-blow account. Then I want you to ask that person to play the pass-it-forward game with someone else, and to keep it going till at least a dozen people are involved."

That was the extent of Neuwirth's intervention, but it started a "cascade of aspirational dialogue among the staff in the ER," he told us. Several days later, he went back down to the ER. The director pulled him aside to ask what he'd done to the troublesome clinician. "He's completely changed. He's positive, on top of things, and is acting like the man in charge (which he was). He's doing a great job, and people are responding wonderfully and talking about some ideas for improvement," the ER director beamed.

About a month later, Neuwirth was working in the
ER admitting a patient to the medical floor. "The
climate was so different you could almost feel it—like
a change in temperature," he told us. Within a few
months, patient satisfaction scores in the ER had
soared from the bottom third to the top third.

LEARNING A NEW LANGUAGE

"Someone told me I was doing organization
development work," he recalls, "and I didn't know
what that was. I figured I'd better find out."

Neuwirth started reading about the topic, and if the
methods made sense, he put them into practice.
He was particularly taken with the work of Robert
Fritz, an internationally recognized organizational
consultant, who taught him the power of the creative
process and the importance of outcome-oriented
thinking as opposed to the oscillating, reactionary
problem-solving approach often deployed by
organizations.

Over the next few years, Neuwirth added community
organizing, social movements, and leadership
to his self-education program—even studying
improvisational techniques as a way to understand

collaborative dialogue in the workplace. He also began consulting with health care groups all over the country, sharing what he had learned.

Neuwirth left Lenox Hill in 2003 to move with his wife, Lisa Davidson, also a physician, to Boston, where she took up an infectious-disease fellowship at a university hospital. He enrolled in a master's program in health care management at the Harvard School of Public Health.

"I needed to learn the language administrators were talking," he told us. "In the past, whenever I went to senior executives in the hospital with ideas for changing and improving the delivery of health care, they would sort of pat me on the head and say I should stick to practicing medicine and teaching— they would run the hospital. I wasn't taken seriously because I didn't speak their language."

During his two years of management study, Neuwirth continued to consult for various health care organizations, specializing in strategic planning, team building, and leadership development. In 2005, he joined Harvard Vanguard Medical Associates, an innovative and progressive provider group that had grown out of an early relationship with the Harvard Medical School and was now a 600-doctor practice. Neuwirth worked as the Chief of Internal Medicine at the group's Kenmore center in downtown Boston, one of 18 locations. In his first couple of months on the job, Neuwirth took it upon himself to interview Kenmore's entire internal medicine team of nearly 80 people.

"I sat down with a notebook," he recalls, "and I told each person that I was going to give them an hour, one-on-one, and I wanted them to tell me, truthfully, how it was going for them and what they thought about the patient care at the practice." He assured them they could speak freely without fear of any consequences, vowing that his only goal was simply to improve things. "The safety part was key," he told us. "If I felt they were holding back because they were nervous about that, I'd get them back for a second hour, close the door, and just listen."

Neuwirth was shocked by what he heard. From the moment they entered the practice, lower-ranked staffers told him, they had felt disrespected. Emotions ran so high that some people actually wept during their interviews. As Neuwirth described the situation: "The nurses weren't talking to the physicians' assistants, who weren't talking to the medical assistants, who weren't talking to the medical secretaries. Everyone pointed fingers at everyone else." The system was flawed, in part because the people equation was askew. Not so dissimilar to other places in which he had worked or consulted, the Kenmore situation was disheartening nonetheless.

> *From the moment they entered the practice, lower-ranked staffers told him, they had been disrespected. Emotions ran so high that some people actually wept during their interviews.*

Neuwirth began to rectify the situation by working to form a tightly knit and progressive management team at Kenmore, one that could lead the charge. He also established a strong co-mentoring relationship with Kenmore's senior administrator, Michael Knosp. Working with Knosp and the rest of his team—David Meenan, Noelle Lawler, Joanne Svenson, Dagmar Eglitis, and Jennifer Whitworth—Neuwirth began to change the culture in the internal medicine department.

First, he sorted people according to their various disciplines and clinical teams, and then he invited each group to lunchtime meetings over pizza, where he prodded the warring factions to ask each other questions, such as: "What are the main problems you face?" and "What can I do to help you?" Neuwirth only had two rules: Every single person in the room had to have a chance to speak without interruption, and people were required to ask questions of each other before they offered rebuttals or comments.

PEOPLE ARE THE KEY TO PROCESS

As one might imagine, the Kenmore staff wasn't used to having this kind of conversation. Moving gradually from doubt to interest, Neuwirth's colleagues began opening up. "They had never heard each other's perspectives before," he said. "On their own, they began to talk and work together in a very different way." A year after Neuwirth arrived, Kenmore's internal medicine staff went from having the system's worst patient satisfaction scores to having one of the best.

Traditionally, he points out, patient dissatisfaction would have been met with a seminar on improving communications or some kind of customer-service program. "What we focused on was simply creating respect and dignity among the staff," he said, "and that alone created a much more respectful and dignified environment for the patients."

In reengineering, the focus is usually on the technical work flows and the process of change itself, which means pulling out the project management charts, time studies, and flow diagrams. In this case, the process of serving patients had broken down, in large part, because of poor relationships within the internal medicine staff. Having approached the problem without a preconceived notion of how to solve it, Neuwirth quickly saw that people were the key. He then developed a way to improve their communication and relationships, thereby improving process performance dramatically.

The foundation for improving patient satisfaction had been laid before Neuwirth arrived at Harvard Vanguard when several clinical and administrative leaders took up the cause. One critical component of their initiative was the formation of tight-knit clinical teams aimed at improving the patient-physician relationship while also supporting the doctor in providing seamless acute, preventative, and chronic care. Each doctor worked with a physician's assistant trained and licensed to treat patients under the doctor's supervision, a nurse, a designated medical assistant, and a medical secretary.

Neuwirth was impressed by the concept of patient-centric teams as well as by the teams themselves. But during his initial interviews, Neuwirth had heard numerous complaints about the doctors' treatment

of their teams—and some complaints from the
doctors, as well. One physician, for example,
described his medical secretary as "an idiot." When
Neuwirth talked with the woman, he discovered that
she had a master's degree in English literature and
spoke and wrote fluently in five languages.

Physician engagement was critical, Neuwirth
realized, because a major part of improving patients'
experience of care depended on the doctors. "The
physicians should be the leaders in the group,"
he told us, given that the entire medical team is
centered around the work of the clinician who sees
the patient. But the doctors showed little interest
in what they saw as just another administrative
reorganization effort, threatening to derail
Neuwirth's people-focused initiatives.

To engage the physicians, Neuwirth chose to focus
on their performance as leaders, and he produced
data from their clinical teams to back it up. "The only
way they're going to learn and develop is if we give
them some feedback about how they're performing
as leaders of their clinical teams," he told staff
members, "and the best feedback will come from
you, the people who work with the doctors on a day-
to-day basis."

Neuwirth enlisted about a dozen people—nurses, medical secretaries, technicians, physicians' assistants—to help him devise a physician leadership survey with questions their fellow team members would be asked to answer. "Who better," he reasoned, "than the people who work side-by-side with the physicians? No one else knows the situations and issues the team encounters as well as the team itself." Presenting the concept as a way to support the physician leaders and help them improve their patient care, Neuwirth asked the group to write on sticky notes what the physician leaders should be doing well and what they weren't doing well. After sorting the hundred or so notes into six categories, each category was boiled down to five questions.

Neuwirth then assembled all of the staff members on the doctor-headed teams and announced that they would participate in an annual survey of their doctor's behavior. He gave each team a list of 30 questions that scored the doctors' treatment of team members and patients in terms of flexibility, follow-up, management skills, communication, patient-centeredness, preparation, and the like. "Essentially," he told us, "the exercise turned into a survey with six themes, and we just attached a Likert scale and handed it out to the six or seven people each doctor worked with on a daily basis." The doctors got anonymous, quantitative feedback that could be tracked over time and allowed for peer comparison.

"We had a patient-centered team leadership score for each doctor," Neuwirth said, "and we could show them how they compared to their peers overall, as well as on the six separate categories. Michael Knosp, David Meenan, Noelle Lawler, and I went over the survey with each doctor and discussed what they could work on and what their team could help them with." And by combining the data, Neuwirth was able to come up with a score for the entire Kenmore site.

When the survey was repeated a year later, it showed a 9 percent increase in the doctors' patient-treatment scores—a significant gain according to health care survey experts with whom Neuwirth shared the findings. And even though Neuwirth left the Kenmore site in 2007 to become Harvard Vanguard's Vice President of Clinical Effectiveness and Innovation, the medical teams have continued the survey. "It's clearly stuck in that organization," he told us.

And that alone is a victory worth noting—it's hard to get this type of introspection to take hold in any enterprise.

TURNING FROM PEOPLE TO PROCESS

During his first months with Harvard Vanguard, Neuwirth had an insight that reshaped his approach to health care delivery: "I realized for the first time that medical assistants and medical secretaries actually run the practice, controlling communication and coordination, while the doctors, nurses, and physician assistants deal with patients in the exam room." So he set up a community-organizing series of lunches with the assistants and secretaries.

"If there is a lever that can actually transform health care," he told them, "you're it. The doctors and nurses are consumed with providing clinical care to the patient. They are caught up in the technical details of medical care, as they should be. You see the flow of things and the bigger picture. You have the power to really transform the practice for the better, but you need to become more proactive and engage more with the practice." Their pride and dignity bolstered, the assistants and secretaries began to act much more professionally, Neuwirth told us. "Their capabilities were amazing, and it was wonderful to see how well they could function without any additional training. They began to act like leaders."

It wasn't enough. The basic health care delivery system was still misfiring; the work flows and processes still needed to be redesigned. Everyone was saying that things were great now that "we weren't sniping at each other anymore," Neuwirth told us, but it wasn't true. The doctors were working overtime and weekends and still not getting their charts done. Both patient- and doctor-satisfaction scores were far too low. Having improved the people aspect of health care delivery, Neuwirth now began to focus on the process side.

He asked for two physician volunteers to study practice work flows, and he formed two teams of observers. The teams ran six-hour time-and-motion studies on two internal medicine physicians while they were seeing patients. The results were shocking. "These were two highly skilled doctors passionate about their patients and passionate about patient care," he told us. "But they were spending only 30 percent of their time in the exam room doing what they love, practicing medicine. Two-thirds of the time was spent on data entry and data retrieval, and exam prep—locating missing data, equipment, and so forth."

By following the doctors around, stopwatch in hand, and conducting follow-up interviews, Neuwirth and his team pieced together a clear, but none-too-pretty, picture of their work. Appointments were so closely booked that a single late-arriving patient could throw off the entire schedule for the day. The doctors were so pressed for time that they couldn't stop after examining a patient to write up their notes. And because they always finished late and wanted to get home to their families, they put off writing up the notes until 9:00 or 10:00 P.M.—seldom finishing before falling asleep.

On weekends, they had 20 or 30 charts to catch up on, a near impossibility that often meant dozens of incomplete charts piled up at the end of the month. "This was not safe medical practice, nor was it healthy for the doctors," Neuwirth said. "All these unwritten charts were like a sword hanging over the doctors' heads. They knew they had to get to them, but when?"

With the research results in hand, he started a series of lunchtime training sessions with the doctors' team members. Neuwirth taught them the basics of process improvement, from how to identify the root causes of a specific problem to developing countermeasures and assigning responsibility for various tasks to the appropriate team members. The medical assistants and supervisors, in particular, were brilliant students, he told us. "They got it faster than I could say it."

The teams came up with all sorts of solutions. To eliminate the note-taking backlog, for instance, they stopped scheduling patient examinations back-to-back. Instead, they reordered the work, leaving free a five-minute block of time between patients so doctors could write their notes while the information was fresh in their minds. Aside from assuring greater accuracy in the notes themselves, the doctors were able to reclaim the time previously spent going back through the files to refresh their memories before laboriously reconstructing the examinations.

Eventually, the teams identified 12 actions the doctors took during a typical patient visit that could be handed off to one or another team member. The doctors were looking up lab results, for example, or searching for equipment that was not readily available,, or actually leaving the examination room to get needed materials or information—all of which could be handled by other team members before or during a patient visit.

Once the work was redesigned from a process flow perspective, the practice was transformed. "I did some time with a stopwatch during the initial observations," Neuwirth related, "and I couldn't believe how frustrating and stressful the doctors' days were. It was actually sort of depressing." Six weeks later, the teams repeated the observations. This time, the doctors were able to be doctors and spend quality time with their patients.

Watching how the physicians and their teams worked after the process redesign was like watching a well-choreographed ballet," Neuwirth told us. "It was a thing of beauty."

PILOTING UNDER THE RADAR

Neuwirth's pilot project won frontline praise but topside disapproval, in part because it bumped up against other major change efforts going on within the larger organization. It wasn't the first time Neuwirth had run into institutional inertia, nor would it be the last. Any attempt to spark serious, in-depth process change will inevitably run into opposition from powerful homeostatic forces within a system that is comfortable with the status quo.

Any attempt to spark serious, in-depth process change will inevitably run into opposition from people comfortable with the status quo, no matter what the organization.

Worse yet, Neuwirth was advocating a radically
different approach to health care delivery and its
organizational management. Instead of the typical
centralized approach, where senior level people
sit in a corporate conference room planning and
deciding what everyone else will be doing, Neuwirth
had inverted the politics and the process of
organizational transformation through the intimate
engagement of frontline clinicians and staff. He had
given them the tools to create change, using a rapid
prototyping approach that produced better results in
a matter of days or weeks, rather than months.

But unable to win over enough senior managers,
Neuwirth responded by taking his change initiative
under the radar screen. With the help of an outside
consultant, he created a 12-hour training program in
process redesign. To avoid conflicting with clinical
office hours and the other major initiatives then
under way, his six two-hour sessions were conducted
before the workday began at a half-dozen sites within
Harvard Vanguard. They ran at two-week intervals to
give participants a chance to implement what they
had learned.

At the Burlington practice site, an initial process
redesign project showed such promise that
every department got involved. Teams engaged
with each other and with redesign, leading to

cross-fertilization. Pediatricians, for example, were observing lab operations and discovering where in the process their lab orders were getting hung up. Lab technicians were looking in on radiology and realizing how they could better work together to provide more streamlined and effective patient care.

A redesign executive-steering team was formed at the Burlington practice and different departments at the site reported on their progress at monthly meetings. "It became a part of the culture," Neuwirth said, "and they just continued to redesign." At one such meeting, he heard a doctor describe a problem his team had encountered—and solved. A patient had phoned in with a question the medical assistant couldn't handle, and unable to connect with anyone at the nurses' station, the assistant had to walk across the building to find a nurse who was free to take the call. When the assistant got back to her desk to make the transfer, she discovered that the patient had hung up before the call could be transferred. A survey revealed that hundreds of similar calls were disrupted just this way every month, causing enormous frustration for patients who frequently had to call back, and enormous rework for the nursing staff.

To remedy the problem, the nurses were moved into a room next to the medical assistant's office, and part of the wall in between was demolished, creating a large window. Now, a medical assistant can simply signal a nurse to pick up the phone before the call is lost, while reassuring the caller that someone will soon provide an answer. The process was repaired, and the number of disrupted calls dropped to only a handful each month.

"WE'RE GOING TO GET IT DONE"

Though Neuwirth's various initiatives often overlapped, a watershed event in the recent reengineering history of Harvard Vanguard was named the LEAD Project. It was designed to restructure the patient-visit process at the system's Chelmsford site and was underwritten by Blue Cross/Blue Shield of Massachusetts in recognition of the need to transform health care delivery so as to elevate the quality of care and keep costs down.

The project involved an intense and radically different change initiative. Normally, such a transformation takes many months of planning, with time set aside for testing and perfecting elements of the redesign. In this case, only 42 days elapsed from the first team meeting to the completion of six major changes and dozens of smaller ones.

Once the situation was analyzed and specific
process changes agreed to, all modifications were
immediately prototyped. "It's going to be down and
dirty," Neuwirth told the teams, "and it's not going to
be perfect. We're going to get it done, and then we'll
build off it and improve the prototype."

With patient experience and the flow of value to the
patient as the drivers, walls were torn down and new
computer systems were installed to streamline the
check-in and check-out processes. Meanwhile, a
multidisciplinary clinical team instituted profound
changes in the patient-care process.

Another distinguishing feature was that the design
team was not limited to doctors, nurses, and senior
administrators. At Chelmsford, the teams of medical
assistants, nurses, and doctors went through the
usual open dialogue Neuwirth had instituted at the
Kenmore practice. "You leave your badge at the door
and focus on doing what's right for the patient, not
your title, advanced degrees, or ego," as he put it.

The project greatly improved patient satisfaction
scores and opened the administration's eyes to
the potential of rapid frontline-directed process
redesign. Dr. Gene Lindsey, the visionary and
forward-thinking CEO of Harvard Vanguard and
Atrius Health, couldn't help but be impressed. He

adopted the engagement and process-redesign approach that Neuwirth had introduced into the LEAD Project as the company's strategic model for the next several years.

Health care CEOs from a number of other Massachusetts-based provider organizations involved in the LEAD Project were blown away by the physician and staff engagement and the enthusiasm apparent as the Chelmsford practice transformed itself before their eyes.

From Neuwirth's perspective, one of the most significant contributions of the LEAD project was the conceptual barriers that it broke and the platform this set for the future of health care delivery. One of these barriers was the age-old belief that health care only takes place in the exam room. Emerging from the LEAD project at Chelmsford was the idea of a "between visit" space—that the vast majority of health care could actually occur where the patient lived, worked, played, and socialized. Neuwirth expanded upon this idea by conceptualizing a paradigm of care where the locus was no longer just within the doctor's office, but rather as part of a larger, integrated, community-based network of health care. This new paradigm of networked care, Neuwirth envisions, would also include patients as the drivers and reengineers of change in health care delivery.

EMERGENCE

The results of the LEAD Project and the growing grassroots interest in Neuwirth's reengineering pilots throughout the Harvard Vanguard organization began to draw notice. In early 2009, he was asked by CEO Lindsey and his senior management colleagues to design and construct a large-scale process-improvement effort based on the methodology he had been piloting since his early days at Kenmore.

Realizing that this was more than a technical process issue, Neuwirth developed and organized a strategic, operational, and cultural redesign effort—a "transformational construct for change"—that has become the operating platform for Harvard Vanguard. In fact, over the past year and half, Harvard Vanguard has become one of the leading adopters across the nation of lean management methods. Neuwirth manages and leads this effort, which now includes nearly a dozen large-scale clinical and operational project redesigns focusing on topics spanning better care for patients with diabetes to reducing unnecessary hospital readmissions to improving the care of the elderly.

Now, Neuwirth told us, reengineering is indelibly imprinted on the culture of Harvard Vanguard. It's the "overarching platform" from the perspective of operations, finance, quality improvement, human resources, strategy, and training, he said. The change is visible everywhere. "People are talking about dialogue, engagement, working together," he told us. "People from different professional backgrounds, different sites, and different departments are working together and making improvements. Frontline people, those closest to the work and the patient, are contributing their ideas." And that represents a radical departure from the past, when what Neuwirth calls a "roll-out, roll-over mentality" was the norm. Now people and leaders from all corners of the organization are engaged in the process of change and the process of continuous care improvement.

On the day we visited, members of the cytology lab department reported on a rapid improvement event—their effort to reduce the rate of errors in pap smear testing. The preparation and labeling of the smears proved to be the core issue. Errors were creeping in because of the way specimens and slides were matched and labeled. Defects and errors were lowering the quality of patient care, and do-overs were raising the lab's costs.

We listened as a half-dozen cytology staffers laid out the problems—and the possible ways to fix them. Step by step, they built on each other's observations. The staff had concluded that too many manual matching steps in between the labeling of specimens and the production and labeling of the related slides were inviting errors.

We were struck by the inclusiveness of the discussion. Everyone from lab supervisor to administrative assistant was involved in coming up with a solution. Besides their active discussions, they used a gap-analysis technique in which everyone stepped back and spent time thinking independently. They wrote down their thoughts on sticky notes, and a facilitator sorted the notes into categories for future reference.

In the end, the cytology people created a new process in which the technicians label a vial and a slide at the same time and place them both into a processing carrier. The *pièce de résistance* was the group's redesign of the vortexing machine to allow processing both vial and slide without removing them from the carrier. Finally, they redesigned the work itself, assigning three-person teams to specimen processing—two people handling the actual work while the third manages the inevitable interruptions that introduce errors.

"Gene Lindsey says the organization is on a vastly different and positive trajectory as a result of the Kenmore transformation, the LEAD Project, and the introduction of this disciplined and widespread approach using Toyota Lean," Neuwirth added. "The other Atrius groups have already begun to send their doctors and administrators to us and are rapidly embracing the process-improvement movement afoot at Harvard Vanguard."

Indicative of the change percolating through Atrius was the response Neuwirth received from a group of executives when he spoke to them recently about the need to make the organization a center of excellence in health care-delivery innovation. "I did not expect them to embrace the idea. Quite honestly, I was worried they would blow it off," he told us. "Imagine my shock when their first question was: 'How much money do you need?' It's a tribute to Gene's leadership and to the other CEOs and chief medical officers' own transformation and development—and an indication of how far the organization has come in a relatively short time."

In our conversations with Neuwirth, we often found ourselves challenged to rethink our own ideas. At one point, for example, he described his approach as "respectful," because every person is treated as more than just someone punching a clock and doing a job. They are individuals with "eyes and ears and a brain, and with perspectives and aspirations and potential." Respect, Neuwirth points out, isn't just about treating people nicely. It's about challenging people to think, grow, and develop—to help them move from a reactive problem-solving mode to a solutions- and outcomes-oriented approach. In the interactions that arise from that approach, he said, it becomes a "communal activity that changes the existing relationships—those people have with their co-workers, their work, and, most importantly, with their patients."

Medical education tends to breed individual operators, and although clinicians are trained to be team players, the concept of team is often restricted to a very few players. Thus, broad-scale teamwork has traditionally been lacking in hospitals and medical practices. But as Neuwirth suggested, reengineering represents a new social contract. It calls for mutual respect along with an understanding that everyone's work is up for examination and potential redesign. The community takes precedence over the individual, and the new social contract goes on to inspire lasting behavioral change.

Reengineering calls for mutual respect along with an understanding that everyone's work is up for examination and potential redesign. The community takes precedence over the individual, and the new social contract goes on to inspire lasting behavioral change.

In his work, Neuwirth told us, he also emphasizes that the goal is not to solve a single surface-level problem but to create a new and better way of working that changes the underlying patterns and processes. A problem may ignite a process redesign, but it should not limit the scope of that process. "You have to transcend the problem," he said, "and build something new and powerful, a new underlying structure that will help move health care forward."

Imagine the difference if thousands of health care organizations, from tiny to vast, from Augusta, Maine, to Alameda, California, got a few big things right. Once pioneers like Zeev Neuwirth show what reengineering can do and how to make it happen, the floodgates will open and change will wash over the nation. You have to believe it. We do.

CHAPTER 3

HARNESS TECHNOLOGY

Anyone who still doubts the value of technology in health care should meet Scharmaine Lawson-Baker, a dynamic nurse practitioner who was running a geriatric practice in New Orleans when Hurricane Katrina struck. Her office was inundated with five feet of water, and all her papers were destroyed, including her patients' medical records.

Several of the 100 people she cared for—homebound and mostly indigent—died in the storm or its immediate aftermath. Like Lawson-Baker herself, some of the survivors relocated to other counties and states, and they began calling her for help. Their new doctors and pharmacies needed to know about their medications, allergies, and lab test results—all the vital information in those records lost in the storm.

Amazingly, Lawson-Baker was ready with the answers. Long before Katrina, she had taken the precaution of entering her patients' contact information and key medical data in her Palm Pilot, which survived the storm intact. Resettled in San Antonio, Texas, she began calling patients herself to pass along the data.

When she returned to New Orleans in the fall, she picked up where she had left off, setting up a new clinic in a house she cleaned and painted herself. Now, though, Lawson-Baker was often making house calls on "four or five old people banded together in a single home, desperately trying to take care of each other."

In urgent need of funds, Lawson-Baker called the Healthcare Information and Management Systems Society (HIMSS), a nonprofit organization dedicated to supporting the use of health information technology to improve health care. HIMSS was scheduled to hold its annual conference in New Orleans in 2006. Maggie Lohnes, the Administrator for Clinical Information Management at MultiCare Health System in Tacoma, Washington—who we will meet later—was in New Orleans scouting for possible off-site visits for convention delegates when she found Lawson-Baker's clinic and heard the amazing story of her and her Palm Pilot.

Soon the story was picked up by the media, contributions came rolling in, and sponsors appeared. It took time, but Lawson-Baker has established a successful nonprofit practice that serves hundreds of the neediest people in New Orleans. Technology can help do that, and more, for health care providers.

In fact, medicine today is basically a product of technological advancement.

In fact, much of medicine today is a product of technological advancement. Before the X-ray ushered in contemporary diagnostic tools and scientists discovered biotechnology, doctors could do little beyond making rough repairs to obvious injuries and soothing patients with their calm authority. These days, technology promises to revolutionize the entire health care field, with innovations ranging from robotic surgery and digitized medical recordkeeping to gene-based therapies and the regeneration of human organs.

When it comes to reengineering health care delivery, it's vital to remember that technology is only an enabler. Care will be improved only if the work is carefully thought through, the technology fully integrated into the total system, and the care providers thoroughly trained in both the processes and the technology.

When it comes to reengineering health care delivery, however, it's vital to remember that technology is only an enabler.

The story of the MultiCare Health System illustrates how to do just that by embracing the challenges and benefits of implementing an electronic health record it calls "MultiCare Connect."

GIVING CARE

Maggie Lohnes is a registered nurse who had spent a decade working in intensive care. But when she realized how technological advances were changing medicine, she saw greater potential for helping others through automation rather than caring for patients directly. "This is my way of giving care," she told us.

In 2006, Lohnes left her job at Huntington Memorial Hospital in Pasadena, California, where she worked to convince physicians of the benefits of electronic health records. Now she feeds her passion for technological caregiving at MultiCare Health Systems in Tacoma, which she describes as "unusually proactive in the adoption of electronic health records," EHR for short. As far back as 1998, MultiCare led the way in Washington state by selecting software from Epic Systems to help automate its ambulatory clinic records.

In 2001, MultiCare's leaders involved all levels of staff, as well as providers and patients, in forging the long-term vision for MultiCare. In a series of conferences called Multivision, the participants tried to look ahead 10 years to determine where health care was heading and what MultiCare needed to do to stay ahead of the curve. Over the course of multiple sessions involving hundreds of people, a mission and vision for the system was articulated.

As a result of those meetings, MultiCare decided to expand its electronic health record throughout the organization, laying the foundation for the technological innovation that infuses the MultiCare Health System today.

The MultiCare Health System mission, "quality patient care," is simple yet profound. The vision is more complicated. Chang freely admits that MultiCare's revenue-cycle and information-management processes needed improvement: "There were three hospitals and multiple clinics at the time, and we had different information systems that didn't talk to one another."

Chang recalled discussions about how to create a seamless, easy-to-access, valued, and sustainable health care-delivery system "that would enhance the experience of our patients, providers, caregivers, and employees." Technology became the tool for melding together the disparate health care processes in multiple locations with the guiding principle of "One Patient, One Record." Chang noted that this concept animated the MultiCare strategy from the beginning, although it didn't win immediate board approval.

Finally, in 2004, this proposal was endorsed by the hospital's Board.

Not everyone was enthusiastic at the beginning. It would be rare if there weren't some pushback from various constituencies. But as the MultiCare Connect project advanced, problems were identified and solved and the technology improved. Lohnes related that over time there were fewer complaints from users. MultiCare had another advantage, she told us: its Tacoma Family Medicine residency program in partnership with the University of Washington included young, eager residents. These residents were immediately enthusiastic about the system, and they provided firm support. One other advantage is that MultiCare began offering its electronic health record to community providers using an application service provider model. Its branded community health record is called "Care Connect." With each new clinic implementation, MultiCare has learned how to effectively and efficiently implement its electronic health record at additional ambulatory sites. Now whenever MultiCare acquires a new practice or signs up a new community practice, it can automate these practices successfully without delay.

At this juncture, computerized physician order entry (CPOE) is fully operational at the three MultiCare hospitals on the Tacoma campus and all of the

ambulatory and urgent care sites. All the ambulatory
orders are online, as are 95 percent of all acute care
orders. Exceptions are limited to emergency (code
blue and trauma) events, downtimes, and a small
number of faxed perioperative orders. In fact, the
ambulatory and urgent care environments are
totally paperless. In the acute care setting, almost
all of the clinical documentation is also online and
available to providers wherever they can access
the internet. Lohnes noted that the only handwritten documentation includes anesthesia records
entered during surgery, some consent paperwork,
or system downtime. Beginning in 2009, MultiCare
also implemented an integrated bedside bar-coded
medication administration system in three of its
four hospitals to improve medication safety. Lohnes
noted that the MultiCare Health System is now
functioning at what's called by HIMSS as a "level six"
for electronic health record adoption, on its way to
the highest level of health information technology
use or "level seven," an entirely paperless electronic
health record everywhere that uses information from
the record to improve health care quality.

There's still work to be done on the document-
imaging piece, Lohnes explained. "Although our
ambulatory medical record is entirely paperless,
right now, our acute care records are a hybrid of
the electronic record, and a small paper chart that

is used to keep track of paperwork collected from outside, some consent forms, and the few remaining paper forms. We are looking at every remaining piece of the paper record to see if it's something that can be interfaced from an outside computer system, whether it can be produced within our electronic health record or if it needs to be scanned into the electronic health record as we move towards an entirely paperless record. . We are really trying to minimize scanning as we move to a paperless record everywhere," she said.

MultiCare's patients can access their electronic medical record via their own patient portal called "MyChart Powered By MultiCare." As more and more patients learn the convenience of accessing their records directly there are many fewer requests for copies of lab tests. MultiCare's Health Information Management Department still provides this service, Lohnes said, but the demand is dwindling. Patients can also see the results of imaging studies, review their immunization history, scheduled vaccines, and medication list , and schedule appointment dates and time.

▶ *Get ready for the changeover.*

MultiCare's success in deploying its EHR can be attributed in large part to its extensive preparation. Early in the process, MultiCare's leaders took four key actions that should serve as lessons for successful implementation. It established:

1. A clear vision of care delivery in the future and how it would evolve.

2. The capability to develop its people, learning, and organizational effectiveness.

3. A service-line strategy.

4. An IT strategy and IT competence.

"We were trying to look at the process from every perspective," Chang told us, "beginning with what health care should be and where we needed to go from that point forward for the next 10 years." And when she says "every perspective," she means it. "We looked at it from a revenue cycle perspective— how could we improve our financial performance? How could we create a learning organization? How could we continue to grow our care line services and develop a center of excellence? How could we use technology to execute our mission and vision, and how could we use that to sustain our financial performance?"

From top to bottom, the organization stresses the importance of its mission to provide quality patient care. So when the Multivision effort began, Chang told us, "we made our mission the true foundation for our core strategies. We developed the care lines, and that allowed us to grow and expand, taking us to the next level. Our integrated electronic health record supports the patient's safety and quality." Everything traces back to the mission.

One of the major reasons MultiCare is successful, Chang declared, is that intense focus on the patient. "The implementation of electronic health records is not information technology's initiative; it's a mission-centered patient initiative."

▶ *Establish guiding principles.*

Implementing and establishing an EHR system takes a long time. MultiCare spent 10 years on an arduous journey that had no lack of challenges, breakdowns, and course changes. During difficult periods, you will need a bedrock belief that guides you in your decision making and helps sustain your efforts. Develop a set of principles that will stand the test of time and return to those to remind your organization of your objectives, the critical outcomes that you want to accomplish, and the high values that you share.

For inspiration, we've included MultiCare's six project goals:

1. Improved patient safety.

2. Assured access to correct patient data for caregivers and administrators.

3. Guaranteed accuracy of the data contained in the record.

4. Simplified, optimized, and consistent processes across the organization.

5. Adoption of the EHR system by every physician and clinician.

6. Better financial performance.

The goals are accompanied by ground rules that start with the admonition to "have fun" and end with "appreciate the experience we all bring to the project." In between are 11 more behaviors such as sharing responsibility for achieving the goals; focusing on issues, not people and emotions; and making decisions based on the guiding principles that are aimed at keeping the project on track.

Chang told us that every time there is a debate going on about how to proceed, "we fall back on the guiding principles, which, by the way, everyone involved in the project had to sign on to." The principles are particularly helpful when you go live, she said, "because issues arise that will have to be prioritized. We use the principles as evaluation criteria."

Your ground rules will obviously reflect your organization's character, but words and phrases like balance, respect, and learning from the past are commonsense admonishments that would suit just about any such undertaking.

▶ *Engage clinicians in design and implementation.*

Building and implementing an EHR system should be more than just an IT project, more than a decision to install a new piece of technology. Technology, after all, is merely an enabler that helps you achieve your ultimate objectives. And in this case, your objective must be to change your hospital's or practice's clinical and administrative processes so that the EHR system will be able to deliver all it promises.

It won't be easy.

The annals of large information technology projects are littered with implementation work that ran up large costs and time overruns yet were never implemented. Why? Because the projects' leaders failed to engage the end users of the technology

systems early in all stages of the implementation.
Such failures are well known and documented,
but even savvy leaders can get caught up in large
IT projects that seem to take on a life of their own.
And when that happens, the projects often end up
dead on arrival because the reality of how real work
needed to change was ignored.

New technology will fail or prove inefficient unless its
users feel comfortable with it. And post-installation
training alone won't turn people into ardent users
of a new system. It's critical, therefore, to engage
clinicians early in the design and implementation of
EHR systems. Physicians must see and experience
these projects as integral to their work. They must
be involved early in the technology's design and in
discussions about how to integrate the technology
with work procedures.

New technology will fail or prove inefficient
unless its users feel comfortable with it.

Dr. Matthew Eisenberg, a pediatrician who came
to MultiCare in 2007 as its Medical Director for
Information Services, told us that MultiCare
first hired a consultant to help learn about and
implement a physician-adoption methodology.
Out of that initiative grew a physicians' information

technology advisory board and a governance model aimed at opening channels of communication. Physicians were recruited to work directly on the implementation project to help merge software, clinical content, and workflows. Eisenberg told us his role "was to bring new energy, strong communication skills, and greater engagement based on the original model. Understanding the value to providers of any new technology was one of the key issues. Next, most important was managing expectations and the resistance to change. Training and strong project management, including a well designed communication plan, round out the physician adoption model. Finally, getting the medical staff leadership on board was critical so that providers could support and manage adoption." The medical staff was invited to workshops to discuss how the EHR system would work, its value, and the expected challenges.

Eisenberg singled out the privately contracted physicians' group that provides emergency services for its adult population. "We have a wonderful relationship with them," he said. "They were obviously quite concerned about the use of new technology and the potential hit to their workflow and productivity. We couldn't ignore that. Plus, we knew that at least half of all our hospital admissions came through the emergency department, so we really needed to partner with them.

"We were able to address some of the key workflow issues and target physicians who needed additional help. We worked together with this group to train and employ scribes to assist some providers with real-time documentation and order entry. Initial funding for the scribe program was provided by MultiCare," Eisenberg told us. "Remarkably, during our first two weeks of the go-live in October, we were able to minimize the decrease in patient volumes to just 3 percent, when everyone had told us that we should expect a 20 to 30 percent reduction over about three months. That cemented our relationship with the group. They understood that in order to be really successful, this needed to be a multidisciplinary partnership between operations and IT," he said.

Eisenberg credits MultiCare's focused and engaged leadership at every level. In addition, MultiCare Health System, under the direction of its executive leadership and hospital board, have implemented gain sharing for all employees. "If MultiCare has a good year, even the person who helps turn over the operating rooms can benefit directly," he said. That keeps everyone in our organization focused on their work and eager to make improvements.

Doctors, nurses, and technicians all have a frontline perspective and experiences that can be crucial in spotting flaws and potential weak spots in new technological systems. The savvy leader of a reengineering project will seek out their advice and adjust to it.

Florence Chang comes at it from another perspective. Know your providers on an individual level, she counsels, if you want to get maximum buy-in.

"Prior to MultiCare," she told us, "I worked as a consultant with a lot of other organizations. But one thing that I always focused on was physician adoption and engagement, because it is critical to the success of electronic health records." She urges that reengineers get their doctors involved in designing the principles so as to identify who are the supporters and who are the naysayers.

She urges that reengineers get their doctors involved in designing the principles so as to identify who are the supporters and who are the naysayers.

"We looked at our community," she went on, "and I contended that liking or disliking EHR or change or technology of any kind wasn't really the issue. It's really about the history a doctor has with the hospital going back 10 to 20 years. That's what causes the

resistance, the pushback that we might potentially
see."

For her part, Lohnes credits MultiCare's original
decision to include frontline staff in the group
of Multivision conferees who were charged with
predicting and planning for future needs. "That
really made them feel a sense of ownership about the
decision to automate," she said.

▶ *Identify champions.*

Leadership, as we've said more than once, is critical
to changing health care delivery. Nowhere is this
truism more apt than in the implementation of
electronic recordkeeping. The enormity of the
change in clinical and administrative work practices
demands that champions man the front line.

Ideally, your champions will be respected members
of the physician community. Their role is not just to
overcome resistance to change, but to demonstrate
how EHR can help improve the lives of individual
physicians and patients, as well as the health care
community. The champions should be enthusiastic
users of the new system and vocal proponents of
process change.

Champions may be found in unlikely places.
Dr. Eisenberg told us that one of the most persuasive

champions of MultiCare's switch to EHR was a doctor in private practice who was heading up the hospital's intensive care unit at the time. This physician worked closely with Eisenberg and his staff on clinical content and workflow issues and was one of their physician super-users in the critical care department at implementation. He and other physicians in his workgroup were so impressed by, and invested in, the EHR project. Soon after when they were looking at changing their practice setting, they decided to join the MultiCare Medical Associates as employed intensivists. These doctors continue to champion the system.

"At MultiCare, we are focused on quality," Eisenberg told us. "That simply stated mission of 'quality patient care' is in the fabric of all of us—and the commitment to leverage information technology to help that along is everywhere." That same passion and engagement extends to the medical staff, he added, and a number of the department chiefs were super-users during the implementation.

▶ *Adopt formal project-management methodologies.*

New technology is never implemented without some headaches, and the bigger the project, the bigger the headaches. An EHR project will be the largest process and technology undertaking most hospitals or physicians' practices will ever undertake. When implemented correctly, it will touch most administrative and clinical processes; engage large numbers of clinicians, administrators, support staff, and technologists; take multiple years to implement fully; and cost a bundle.

Cost overruns and delays in implementation are all too common. But accepted management methodologies can help you get your project done right. We strongly recommend the establishment of a project management office, staffed by full-time clinicians and managers, to oversee both the technology and procedural work. A Web page that makes plans, progress, and breakdowns fully transparent to all participants is a decided plus.

"A project of this size needs the discipline and clear accountability," Chang said. "There were issues and risks that needed to be addressed, and the process of addressing those issues, including budget management, had to be as transparent as possible."

Eisenberg is enthusiastic about the way MultiCare's leaders embraced the importance of a project-management office. "We are blessed to have built a wonderful project management team and a consistent methodology that we try to follow. It works very well," he told us.

The project-management office keeps track of MultiCare's enterprise project priority grid, each one mapped to their organizational goals. At a project level, "We can take the 15 issues that arise at our meetings," Eisenberg told us, "and prioritize them based on the standard scoring method that originated in our very first inpatient go-live back in 2007." From that list, the top three issues are scheduled for immediate attention. Without this sort of project-management discipline, he said, MultiCare's EHR problems and optimization requests would not get the kind of attention they deserve and like so many other organizations that can only say, "we'll get to them when we can."

▶ *Protect physician productivity.*

Most of us tend to assume that new technology is an unmitigated blessing that will perform as advertised. Expectations of both its usefulness and performance can be badly distorted, and there are always unintended consequences of new technology adoption. Health information technology has a spotty record when it comes to improving the work and lives of clinicians. Breakdowns occur when doctors are left out of the loop entirely or when they are included too late to make a real difference. Those mistakes typically occur when the project is seen as *just* an IT undertaking rather than part of a life-changing reengineering process.

MultiCare adopted a formal installation process that included very careful workflow analysis_both the current state and the desired future state. "Front-line physicians and nurses developed the desired future state," Maggie Lohnes told us. "Once the workflows and content were analyzed, we mocked up scenarios in a development system and we asked the doctors, nurses, and other clinical staff to validate it." In Lohnes's opinion, allowing the practitioners to optimize their workflow was one of the keys to getting adoption. "They realized they were partners in this," she said, "which led to a lot of tweaking to improve the system before we went live."

But even when clinicians are engaged early on, it's crucial that they pay special attention to how IT systems and hardware are incorporated into the patient visit. Many physicians worry about poorly designed systems that distract them from patient interaction and slow productivity.

Making sure you understand exactly how the EHR technology will work in the physician's exam room before it's installed is one of the keys to successful implementation of the system.

> *Making sure you understand exactly how the EHR technology will work in the physician's exam room before it's installed is one of the keys to successful implementation of the system.*

MultiCare found many of its physicians feared they'd end up staring at a computer screen during a patient visit instead of paying attention to the patient. Particularly those who considered themselves "more high-touch than high-tech," in Maggie Lohnes's words, had to be shown how to incorporate a computer into a visit without shortchanging patients in an impersonal interaction. One suggestion, she said, was to ask patients if they wanted to see their records on screen. That way, the patients would be engaging with the physician as he or she used the computer, rather than allowing the machine to become a wall that blocked interaction.

Noting that no physician is eager to decrease his or her productivity, Lohnes suggests that "you allow them some latitude during the first few weeks after adoption, giving them time to get comfortable before holding them to their usual output." Once the doctors and nurses become comfortable with the

EHR system, she says, they and you should expect improved productivity. And don't be surprised if that improvement shows up in unexpected ways. One MultiCare physician was quoted happily acknowledging that, "for the first time since starting my practice, I was able to go home and have dinner with my family, knowing that all of my records were completed." Medical practitioners take great satisfaction in being able to produce more on their own. They will increase their productivity levels as soon as humanly possible.

▶ *You can never pay too much attention to detail.*

The number of decisions that must be made in the implementation of an EHR system are almost too numerous to count. Decisions about which technology, what information will be entered and how it will be structured and how tasks will be performed await a consensus view. Operating and governance issues also demand solutions.

Each decision must be carefully taken and differing opinions about choices given due consideration. And above all, you must be sure that the necessary decisions are actually being made. Keep track of the outcomes of all disputes to make sure you are getting closure, and then track the details of design and implementation. Errors or omissions can occur in a host of areas, so vigilance will be critical.

When MultiCare was designing its system, it formed a physician advisory group to help, and also designated full-time and part-time project physicians to engage in the actual work.

Florence Chang told us that as the system was being designed, Dr. Matt Eisenberg and his team took the product to every single physician's office in the community to get their approval. "We did 47 road shows prior to going live," she said. "We took the product to our pediatricians. We took it to every single specialty out there to get their endorsement so that when we went live, we went live with about 350 order sets, every single one approved and endorsed by our physicians' group."

Harry pointed out that going to 47 offices will usually produce at least 40 new requirements, slowing the process of implementation to a crawl. He wondered how Chang managed to get endorsements rather than demands for something new.

"You're right," she replied, "going to so many different sites will usually increase the number of requests. But from the beginning, we developed a guiding principle of providing standardized care to our patients. We wanted to reduce the variation, and we shared with the physicians our concerns about adding instead of eliminating steps that do not increase value."

The physicians responded admirably. In some cases, Chang said, "we had to bring colleagues together to discuss the system's design, reminding them that we were only going to create one system, one order set." They worked it out.

▶ *Train and practice.*

Implementing an EHR system will affect the work of hundreds, if not thousands, of people in your organization. A training program must be developed for every area of your operation that will be affected. Make the training as experiential as possible. Practicing with both the new technology and the redesigned processes will give people more confidence and competence in their work, while also showing them how their lives will be improved by the arrival of EHR.

"We did very personal shoulder-to-shoulder work," Maggie Lohnes told us. "I had these great relationships with physicians, and I'd tell them that they got into medical school so they could learn how to incorporate computers into their workflow. And since they are used to using those minimally invasive tools during surgeries, they could certainly handle a mouse." Helping them side-by-side, one-by-one didn't eliminate the learning curve, she added, but it did help their practices.

"Another great training program," she said, "was aimed at MultiCare's employed physicians. During the years of go-live, we set aside part of their work schedule for class time and practice sessions with the computers. It was a cost well spent."

▶ *Go with big bang implementation, but plan extensively.*

There is a valid debate that comes with every large technology project: Should it be implemented in phases, or should the switch be thrown systemwide in one big bang on a single day? The usual argument for a phased approach is that it poses less risk—and if the change is small, that's probably true. A rounds-making robot, for instance, can be tested in a pilot project and modified for missteps before a squadron is sent to roam a hospital's halls.

However, for all-embracing technological projects, such as the implementation of an EHR system, the big-bang approach is actually less risky than a slow rollout. As you begin your design, you'll see how these kinds of projects touch all parts of a hospital's or practice's operations. You might be able to exclude some areas of a hospital's operations initially, but you will then need patches to create connectivity and those patches will have their own risks. For example, if you don't go live with the system in the pathology lab at the same time you bring on the operating suites, paper will have to travel between the locations, slowing processes and creating the potential for errors.

If you have paid adequate attention to detail, training, and practice, we believe the safer option is to go live with a major new system on a single day. But you must have a procedure in place for monitoring and quickly fixing any breakdowns that occur. People are always uneasy when a significant change is implemented, and if there are problems with the technology right out of the gate that aren't fixed immediately, you'll have a hard time winning back their confidence.

MultiCare decided to go big bang because many of its patients travel between the different hospitals and clinics, Lohnes said, "and we didn't want them to have part of their orders on paper and part electronic."

▶ *Realize that the work is never done.*

All successful reengineering efforts have the additional benefit of developing an organization's appetite for change. So prepare for that eventuality from the outset of your EHR project by maintaining the capacity and capability to optimize the new processes you have developed, and then to move on to other areas where reengineering will most improve performance.

In other words, don't let your new skills wither. Leverage the technology and process platform you have built to continue improving clinical outcomes, patient experiences, and your ability to attract an expanding range of customers. When properly used, an EHR is an incredibly valuable asset.

Dr. Matt Eisenberg told us that when visitors come to MultiCare, the team talks about its leadership, its engaging vision, its project-management skills, its training programs, its communications strategy, its well-skilled build team, and the need for implementation that never ends. In short, "we try and model that multi-disciplinary engagement," he says. It's not that hard if you can get people on the same page. But when all is said and done, "You can optimize until you die," he rightly notes. And that's a good thing.

First, as Florence Chang points out, it does pay for itself. She put together a total 10-year cost ownership and return on investment analysis. "We will break even in 2013," she told us, "but you have to have the discipline to continue driving operational change."

The payoff? "I do believe that quality prints money," Chang says. "If you improve the quality of care, you can reduce costs within the health care system. But it does require significant discipline, and you will need to continue optimizing the system and changing the workflow process."

When MultiCare started its project, it had 3,000 different workflows in three hospitals, she said. When it was ready to go live, workflows had been reduced to 1,200, and the numbers continued to drop with each CPOE iteration—and change and modifications continue.

Chang has the last word. "Implementing electronic health records is probably the best thing that can happen to health care because it drives standardization," she said. It forces you to look at your organization from a very different perspective. It magnifies all your broken processes, all the fragmentation within your system. It's up to us how we want to change that. But forget about first trying to change what people think. Concentrate on changing what they do, because the faster we can change what people do, the quicker we can optimize the new process."

> *"Implementing electronic health records is*
> *probably the best thing that can happen to*
> *health care because it drives standardization."*

THE BIG SECURE SYSTEM IN THE CLOUD

Hardly anyone disputes that thousands of lives and billions of dollars could be saved every year if all medical records were available whenever and wherever they were needed. If a man from Idaho were injured in a car accident in Florida, for example, the emergency-room physicians would know his medical history by the time the ambulance arrived at the hospital, and they could prepare accordingly. Even if the victim were unconscious, no time would be wasted on inquiries about drug allergies or pre-existing conditions. Mistakes could be avoided and treatment tailored to the patient's needs.

But deployment of electronic health records for the majority of Americans—a 2004 Bush administration initiative—remains a distant dream, even though Maggie Lohnes told us that "the technology is there. Standards are available. Selecting one and committing to it as a nation is all that is left." But she admits that "the politics of it"—forming a national committee and picking the people to serve—raised concern among different constituents that turned into a nine-month debate on that issue alone. According to the *New England Journal of Medicine,* just 1.5 percent of private hospitals have a comprehensive electronic medical-records system. What's worse, most of the existing systems can't communicate with one another.

The lack of a national system directly affects the quality of U.S. health care and the magnitude of its costs. Both patients and providers spend countless hours filling out repetitive paper forms that must be filed away by the office staff. And the record-retrieval procedure steals more time from practitioners that could be spent with patients.

The Obama administration's 2009 stimulus act included more than $20 billion for health care information technology. The ultimate goal is to improve outcomes and control costs by collecting and sharing health data for better decision-making, while protecting patient privacy.

The United Kingdom began several years ago to build a nationwide, electronic health care records system. Billions of pounds have been spent and success may be within reach. But such an approach requires broad agreement on processes and information standards, and that is very difficult to achieve in countries highly dependent on private health care providers. Another way forward is emerging, however, one based on the creation of a

secure "cloud" into which health care records would
be placed. Search engine technologies could then be
used to locate the right information.

(For the less-sophisticated technology user, a "cloud"
is a seemingly endless array of networked servers
providing on-demand computing to multiple users.
What makes the cloud viable today is the low cost of
computing power, the ubiquitous network provided
by the Internet, the abundance of bandwidth,
and recently developed, sophisticated means for
managing data. The technology world has been
waiting nearly half a century for the convergence of
these capabilities.)

Technology is helping to solve the problem of
creating some form of a national health care-record
repository—virtual or otherwise—but providers need
solutions today. Work must begin locally now, but
we hoist a large warning flag: An electronic health
care-record project will be the largest technological
endeavor a typical hospital or medical group practice
will ever undertake. Done correctly, as we've seen,
it will change almost all clinical and administrative
work, while engaging numerous doctors,
administrators, technologists, and support staff.

> *An electronic health care-record project will*
> *be the largest technological endeavor a typical*
> *hospital or medical group practice*
> *will ever undertake.*

Complete implementation will take many years and cost a lot. Join the movement, but make sure you thoroughly understand the issues and have a well-thought-out plan in place before you begin.

As new technologies like EHR systems are introduced, it is imperative that the three principles we spelled out at the beginning of this chapter are followed: The work must be carefully thought through, the technology fully integrated into the health care-delivery system, and the care deliverers fully trained in both the processes and the technology. Otherwise, not only will you will see a poor return on your investment, but you will risk making the work of physicians less, not more, productive.

A CHECKLIST FOR IMPLEMENTING NEW TECHNOLOGIES

Just as checklists have become an important part of medical protocols, we suggest the following checklist for implementing new technologies focused on the EHR:

- ▶ Have you developed the capabilities and acquired the capacity to implement the new technology? Substantial incremental work is required for the adoption of new technologies. Good systems and process skills are critical for implementing an EHR, and you will need these skills well through adoption. Develop or acquire them early, and build the muscle you need.

- ▶ Have you established a set of principles to guide you through the change journey? No major reengineering effort ever plays out without argument, some second thoughts, and roadblocks. It's important to keep your final objectives in sight and to establish a set of principles that you will follow even when problems intervene. In many ways, these principles serve as a moral compass.

- ▶ Have you engaged the right people in the work redesign effort? We cannot stress how critical work redesign is to the successful implementation of new technologies. The people most affected by the work change must be engaged early in discussions of how their work will be redesigned.

▶ Have you identified the leaders who will shepherd the change? They must exhibit process sensibilities plus an appreciation for what the technology can achieve. And they must demonstrate their own practical use of the technology. With many organizations striving to implement systems, these leaders will be in high demand and increasingly in short supply.

▶ Have you established a governance process to answer questions of policy and oversee the effort? Policy issues almost always accompany a new technology—questions of use, privacy, access. The people implementing a new technology often aren't positioned to answer these questions. An elevated perspective may be required. A governing body of shared and diverse interests is always helpful.

▶ Have you established a project management structure and methodology? It takes exceptional discipline to manage any complex technology or system, and a fulltime staff dedicated to the effort is required. A standard project-management methodology will keep all the parts moving forward together.

▶ Are your project plans sufficiently detailed to allow you to manage all of the parts effectively? Big ideas and big technologies don't get implemented without a lot of attention to detail. You don't want to get lost in the "woods" of your work, but you do want to identify all of the "trees" that will need attention.

▶ Have you established training programs and practice facilities to enable people to become familiar with both the new technology and the new work processes? There is nothing like experience and practice to build confidence in the workability of new technologies and processes and to reduce risk to patients.

Technology isn't the universal solution for reengineering health care, but it's safe to say that technology will be a critical enabler of many reengineering initiatives. That, however, is just the beginning of reengineering, since a technological innovation will inevitably lead to changes in most or all of the processes in place at hospitals, medical groups, and individual physicians' offices. Process changes are the subject of the next chapter.

CHAPTER 4

FOCUS ON
PROCESSES

"We want to generate a new set of ways to meet the needs of patients," says Dr. Victor M. Montori, a professor of medicine at the world-renowned Mayo Clinic.

In reengineering terms, what most concerns Montori are the processes of health care, especially the interaction between patient and doctor, which has barely changed in more than a century. "Medicine has changed, people have changed, technology has changed, but the exam room isn't so different from what it was in the 1800s," according to Dr. Michael D. Brennan, an endocrinologist. (Both Brennan and Montori have been closely associated with the acclaimed SPARC—See, Plan, Act, Refine, Communicate—Innovation Program at Mayo— Brennan as medical director and Montori as director of research and education.)

"Medicine has changed, people have changed, technology has changed, but the exam room isn't so different from what it was in the 1800s."

"Our problem is that we have all the wrong processes in place," agrees Debra Geihsler, a health care executive who has worked to transform major delivery systems in Chicago and Boston, and is now embarking on a new venture in Indianapolis. What's needed, she says, is a set of processes "focused more on prevention and wellness, and less on chronic disease and hospitals."

But how can medical processes, developed and ingrained over decades, be successfully changed? Consider the principles that have emerged from the case studies presented in this book.

▶ Start small and build on proven results.

You cannot reengineer an entire organization in one go-round. The scope and scale of such an undertaking is simply unmanageable. You might map out the overall journey and the steps you will take to complete it over time. But in the beginning, you should concentrate on only a few areas. Start small—not in terms of ambition, but in terms of the number of people you will initially engage in your reengineering project. Look for teams, departments, and practices with a framework for success—clinical leadership, performance issues that make the case for change, and ambitious people who will work hard to make it happen. Once you can demonstrate improved performance, you are ready to broaden your campaign.

We advise you to prove your case first in a small venue for two reasons: The changes will be easier to manage, and clinicians will want to see proof the new care-delivery processes work before they risk the well-being of patients. Conversely, they will gladly adopt a revamped process or procedure if they are shown a better way. As we have said more than once, doctors come to work to do good. The best, most effective, and caring treatment is the one they will choose. Zeev Neuwirth's reengineering efforts have proved the point many times over.

When Neuwirth and his colleagues set out to improve the productivity of the orthopedics department at the Harvard Vanguard Kenmore medical practice, they knew it wouldn't be easy. The practice is filled with outstanding surgeons who are in high demand, making access a problem. Patients wanting an immediate appointment sometimes had to wait days, if not weeks, to be seen. And if a patient had to go outside the practice for care, Kenmore ran the risk of losing the patient altogether. More importantly, if the patient did come back to Kenmore, his or her medical records would be incomplete, requiring numerous error-prone and time-consuming steps to stitch the pieces back together. All in all, a big mess in need of fixing.

Neuwirth and his colleagues instituted a rapid improvement event in which participants typically focus on one process, develop a strategy to increase its efficiency, and then implement the strategy, essentially shutting down the process temporarily until the fixes are in place. Initially, the orthopedics team was not enthused by the prospect. The doctors arrived for the first meeting on Monday morning wearing expressions that declared, "Why are you wasting my time?" But by the end of the week, with the process change in place, they were amazed at what they had accomplished.

"I have learned more this week than I have in the past 30 years of my career," the chief of orthopedics told Neuwirth. "I never knew how much work and all the processes that went on around me." Immersed in his operating schedule and clinical work, this physician never understood just how good his staff was or how dependent they were on other people, particularly the radiology department. "I learned that all the stuff my team does is just as important as what I do," he announced to a stunned audience at the end-of-week project report.

"I never knew how much work and all the processes that went on around me."

Now the chief is a strong advocate of reengineering and has installed his own new process: He joins his orthopedics team every morning and afternoon for five-minute huddles. The whole team huddles

at about 8:00 A.M. to discuss the day ahead, air
any problems, and get answers to a series of set
questions, including: How is every team member
feeling today? At the late-afternoon huddle, the
questions run to how the team functioned that day.
Were there difficulties? Any patient complaints? If so,
were they effectively addressed? How can we avoid
similar problems in the future?

Possibly, the most important change has occurred
within the culture of the orthopedics department
rather than in the work-flow processes alone.
When the chief instituted his process, he gave team
members the freedom to speak out.

The rapid improvement event also formed a strong
bond between orthopedics and radiology. The
two departments are located about 100 feet apart,
and for years orthopedists have sent patients to
radiology. Yet the staff members seldom talked
to one another before the process redesign. But
afterwards, radiology staffers have daily huddles,
too, and they began to stay abreast of orthopedics'
daily management board. In fact, the huddles have
become shared affairs with employees from both
departments intermingling. Neuwirth admits to
having made "tons of mistakes" in the process
redesign effort. "But I think we're getting the big
things right," he says.

One note here: You might be confused by the advice we give here to start small with early process change and the advice we gave you in the previous chapter to go with a big bang implementation for EHR initiatives. If you have not experienced work change in your organization, it's still helpful to start small—giving people the opportunity to experience the benefits of change and to begin the process of behavior adjustments. But once you have built the capability to implement electronic records across your organization, we assume that you have also developed the sensibilities and capabilities to broadly implement work and behavioral change—and that you can move more aggressively.

▶ *Go for quick results but prepare for long adoption times.*

Beginning with a small-scale reengineering effort has the major advantage of producing quick results. Projects that take too long wear people out and make them question the value of their work. A quick result—whether it's improved quality, a lower cost, or a superior patient or physician experience—keeps people in the game. It validates the ideas at the heart of process change and sets the stage for the longer-term efforts needed to perfect a process, particularly when you have larger projects ahead.

Don't make the mistake of starting a reengineering effort by trying to change how people think. It hardly ever works. Cognitive change just takes too long. We believe that changing what people do is the best way to change how they think. Many people must physically experience change before they can see its benefits. So the faster you change how clinical work is done, the faster the behaviors of clinicians and their staffs will change.

> *Cognitive change just takes too long. We believe that changing what people do is the best way to change how they think.*

Dr. Tom Knight, speaking from experience at Houston's Methodist Hospital System, says, "It's not what we say, but what we do. It's what we stand for to some degree, but really it's what we stand behind. Quality and safety in health care cannot be managed. It must be led. It must be inspired. It must be modeled. And, it must be lived." "The good news," he goes on, "is that we have a workforce that will do it." And when it comes to the process of change, "it's a whole new behavioral science."

So changing behavior is the cart behind the horse of proven process improvement. We will tell you more

about how to accomplish behavioral change when
we talk about people.

Following our advice to start small so as to attain
quick results, and then spread process change across
your entire organization, means that a complete
change in the delivery of care will be a long time
coming. Every reengineering effort cited in this
book has taken two to three years to achieve full
implementation. You should expect to spend no less
time on your reengineering project.

▶ *Fix errors and breakdowns, but don't lose sight
of the end game.*

Errors and breakdowns may point to areas in need
of reengineering. But when a problem arises, be
careful about adding more resources and layers of
complexity to solve the problem. That might only
mask the true issues. Solving the immediate problem
and ignoring the underlying issues ends up adding
costs over time, which health care delivery can't
afford if real improvement is the goal.

Look for the systemic causes of your problem and
fix the processes that are creating it. You may have
to invest more time and resources than you initially
expected, but the more-inclusive approach will pay
off in the long run, and you will be assured that the
errors and breakdowns won't reoccur.

We can provide a personal example of how more expansive process-fixing trumps limited problem-solving. A few years ago, the then administrator of the U.S. Veterans Administration (V.A.) asked Jim to assess problems that were delaying the settlement of veterans' health care and disability claims. Some veterans had to wait months, even years, before their claims were settled—and to our everlasting shame, some died before they were paid what they were due.

As a dedicated proponent of reengineering, Jim turned to the principles being applied by businesspeople around the world in hopes of fixing the government's problem. He discovered that several factors were contributing to the breakdown. To begin with, medical cases had become more complex and required more of caseworkers' time. Adding to the delay was the V.A.'s inability to quickly access veterans' service and medical records, which were mostly on paper and scattered across multiple locations. At the time, the V.A. had 80 clerks stationed at the Pentagon whose sole duty was to find the records of veterans needing assistance.

Jim recalls being directed to a well-meaning admiral who had been charged with finding a "solution to the problem." When Jim suggested that the problems could be eliminated if the V.A. adopted new processes and updated its information technology, he was told that the standard approach—hiring extra clerks and caseworkers—was more likely. No heavy lifting would be required since Congress was sympathetic to the plight of veterans and would provide more money to get the job done. Not surprisingly, the traditional "solution" was adopted.

This approach to fixing problems is no fix at all. The truth is that many problems don't really get fixed; they just get buried under more complexity and new resources.

The Veterans Administration has gone a long way toward implementing electronic health care records since Jim was asked to help. But we suspect that some real reengineering is still needed to meet the needs of veterans. If the V.A. asked for help again, our advice would be to go deep, address the systemic issues, and eliminate the problems once and for all.

▶ *Recognize that process change is iterative.*

Once you decide something needs changing, you naturally want to get started, wasting as little time as possible. So you verify the need, think about ways to make it happen, decide which one is preferable, and formulate a plan. You check with the people who will be affected by the plan—customers, employees, suppliers—and if anyone has a serious concern, you make changes accordingly. Then, you push the "start" button. Mission accomplished, you dust off your hands and look for the next problem to solve.

Self-satisfied though you may be, that's the wrong way to make changes, especially big ones meant to transform the way you do business. The right way is to test your ideas and get feedback at every stage, using the information you gather to improve each step in the process and shape the next move. To see the preferred method at work, we need look no further than the SPARC program the Mayo Clinic is using to improve health care by changing the way doctors interact with their patients.

The time-honored ritual in the doctor's office seems designed, consciously or not, to underscore the doctor's authority and the patient's submission to it. The patient waits for the doctor in an ill-fitting gown in a typically chilly exam room. The doctor examines the patient on a high, paper-covered, padded table that resembles the lift at a tire shop. The patient is then told to get dressed and is given license to enter the physician's private office, where he or she receives the verdict from across the doctor's desk.

Small wonder the patient mutely accepts the diagnosis and prescribed treatment, and then forgets the doctor's instructions and winds up taking

only half the pills or swallowing them at the wrong
intervals.

Mayo has been innovating health care since the
clinic was founded in the late nineteenth century.
SPARC is its latest and perhaps most sweeping
attempt to change the patient experience and health
care delivery. On its face, SPARC is an evolving,
experimental patient-consulting center on the
17th floor of the clinic's headquarters in Rochester,
Minnesota. At its core, however, the program
represents a commitment to reengineer every
possible aspect of patient care, ranging from the way
pills are prescribed to patient check-in procedures
and the ethos of exam and operating rooms.

Patients consult their doctors in a variety of
settings, the center's primary goal being to hear
and understand every patient's needs. But Mayo's
practitioners know that whatever concerns a patient
is able to express cover only part of the territory
that must be explored. SPARC researchers view a
consultation using small, inconspicuous cameras
(with patient consent) that allow them to discern
unarticulated needs made apparent by a patient's
reactions and body language. And even deeper,
latent needs are being identified, Dr. Montori says, by
trying new approaches and watching how patients
react. "We hear all the time about a clinician being

empathetic. Now we're watching empathy at work—
the eye contact, the listening. We see the whole
dance."

Actual patient feedback is another critical
component of the SPARC program that provides
clues to a person's real needs, and the feedback
is ongoing. The researchers form their plans in
segments, incorporating patient feedback every step
of the way in a quest for ultimate effectiveness. Each
improvement, in turn, is tested to take advantage of
another round of feedback. In effect, the researchers
use each new variation to shape better questions.

One innovation that grew out of the SPARC program
are the kiosks located around the Rochester campus
and at Mayo facilities in Jacksonville, Florida, and
Scottsdale/Phoenix, Arizona. The kiosks make
it easier for Mayo's 500,000 annual patients to
check in upon arrival. Many of these people find
it difficult to stand in line for check-in, explained
Ryan Armbruster, the program's original director
of operations and design. "The kiosk is similar to
what you'd find at an airport," he said. "You walk
up and enter a little information, and it asks a few
questions about what you're [there] for. It confirms
the information with the front desk, and you can
have a seat."

In its first iteration, the check-in kiosk was deliberately crude and boxy-looking. Patients were left to imagine a functioning terminal with a power supply that would enable them to check in for their clinic appointments. But based on the reactions to that first, very rough sketch, the next version featured a laptop with what appeared to be a touch screen. The screen didn't actually work, but a technician sitting alongside with a keyboard simulated a working prototype by typing in patient responses. The next model had a working touch screen, and the adjustments continued in response to patient feedback until the real thing was in place. It was all part of the rapid prototyping that goes on in the SPARC program in response to patient reactions.

The final product was an immediate hit, with 87 percent of those who tried the kiosk saying they would use it again. And no wonder, since the kiosk was basically designed by its end users.

▶ *Build in patient education.*

All too many years ago, Jim's son, Adam, was born five weeks early. The proud parents were able to take their baby home two days later on a fine Saturday morning in Boston. But here's how Jim remembers the happy, but anxious occasion:

"My wife and I were a bit perplexed about what the future would hold. We had studiously attended childbirth classes, but because Adam arrived early, we missed the classes on caring for a newborn. We knew next to nothing about it, and because it was a weekend, there was no one at the hospital to advise us, and we had no knowledgeable family members nearby.

"Every time the baby cried, we frantically searched through *The Common Sense Book of Baby and Child Care*, Dr. Benjamin Spock's iconic guide, to see what might be the problem. Fortunately, for Adam, we finally hired a part-time nurse who *did* know what to do."

Times change and people change, too. Hospitals now recognize that improving patient care isn't just a matter of rooting out redundant procedures and telescoping tasks. It sometimes means adding a component like patient education that enhances the whole experience far more than its cost might indicate.

Today's patients take it for granted that health care delivery will include sizable helpings of education on myriad topics. They want to know the source of their problems and their treatment options. They also want to know what they can do on their own to live longer and healthier. And studies show that patients

who take part in good education programs have
better clinical outcomes, are more likely to follow
their treatment plans, and are less anxious about
their care.

Cathy Camenga, a nurse with 25 years of experience
in clinical practice, knows all about patient concerns
and the value of good education. She was the
founding director of the Health Education Initiative
at the California Pacific Medical Center (CPMC)
a decade ago. Her program has become the gold
standard for Web-based patient education in the
United States. Such recognition is typical for the
much-honored medical center. In 2009, for example,
CPMC's three campuses were three of the 34 urban
hospitals in the United States recognized as a
Leapfrog Top Hospital for Quality and Safety. This
represents the fourth year of recognition for CPMC.

Camenga was finishing her Master's degree in
Nursing at the University of California at San
Francisco when she was hired by CPMC. "The job
was great," she told us. "It was innovation—process
improvement, really. The assignment was to
spread patient education across a system and the
continuum of care."

At the time, she said, very few materials were
available to inform patients and their families
about particular ailments and treatments or about

the hospital experience in general. Patients being discharged, for instance, would be handed a doctor's note on a prescription pad. But there was no real standardization process for instruction, written or oral, about what to expect at home.

Camenga soon realized that a major part of her job was to win the support of the hospital's doctors. They would have to sign off on any educational materials she distributed—either on paper or through the Web site. What is more, Camenga hoped to convince them to write much of the material. It took some doing, but she succeeded. She advises against contacting doctors in a group e-mail. "They like to be approached one-on-one," she says, adding: "Develop the relationship and bring them along slowly."

Over time, Camenga helped to create what she calls "a culture of patient education and of patient inclusion in the process of care." The patient-centric approach now permeates doctors' practices and the hospital as a whole, and focus groups suggest ways in which it can be improved.

A visit to the CMPC Web site demonstrates the dramatic transformation within the center's caregiving process. Under the heading, "Learning About Your Health," a visitor is offered online materials written not just in English, but in Chinese, Russian, and Spanish, as well. Classes or support groups designed to help people "navigate around problems related to serious diseases such as cancer" can be attended in person or accessed in podcasts.

An alphabetized listing provides online access to dozens of detailed entries prepared by the hospital's clinicians. The topics range from abdominal surgery and how to prepare, what to expect in the hospital, and caring for yourself at home, to upper gastrointestinal issues—specifically, what an upper GI series is and how long it takes to get the exam results.

Jim would have appreciated the advice found under "P" for parenting and infant care. The topics range from sunscreen application to the normal weight loss newborns experience in the first few days after birth.

Cathy Camenga will tell you that successful patient education today requires a major investment in time and resources to achieve excellence in form, content, and delivery. It crosses all areas of a hospital's patient care. In other words, it's not just a handout any more—it's a process that has benefited from reengineering.

▶ *Cope with your chronic customers.*

Many businesses have what could be called chronic customers—people whose needs are great and who won't go away, though filling their needs is simply not profitable for the provider. Businesses can get out of unprofitable lines of work, but that's not an option for health care providers.

For hospitals, the people we are describing are those with chronic diseases who can't seem to monitor their conditions, take their meds, or maintain a healthy lifestyle. They often end up being hospitalized or receiving expensive emergency-room treatment. The patients themselves would much prefer to stay at home—and many health care leaders think that's wise, because it's better for the patients and allows for a better use of medical resources. But teaching chronic patients to cope with their conditions is difficult, time-consuming, and costly.

One solution has come from the so-called disease management industry, which takes over the teaching process and provides programs to help chronic patients care for themselves. These companies primarily employ nurses to phone patients and inquire about their well-being, offering advice and encouragement. Insurance companies and large employers commonly hire the managers to help keep policyholders and employees healthy in hopes of reducing insurance costs. But the effectiveness of disease management by phone is questionable.

In recent years, more sophisticated approaches to chronic-disease management have sprung up. We talked with one of the pioneers in the field, Dr. Cheryl Pegus, general manager and chief medical officer of SymCare Personalized Health Solutions, in West Chester, Pennsylvania. After meeting Pegus, we would be hard-pressed to find a part of the health care business she hasn't improved.

Born in Trinidad and Tobago, Pegus was raised in Brooklyn, New York, received her medical degree from Cornell University Medical College, and did her clinical training in cardiology at New York Hospital-Cornell. Her interest in minority communities led to their greater participation in clinical drug trials, which eventually took Pegus to the corporate side of health care. She accepted posts with Pfizer, LipoScience, and Aetna, and earned a master's degree in public health at Columbia University along the way. At Aetna, she served as national director for women's health and then was named chief strategist for clinical product development.

SymCare provides disease management companies with inTouch, a very sophisticated diabetes treatment program. The system, recently cleared by the FDA for nonprescription use, includes Web-based technology, individual coaching, educational materials, and a rewards program. It automatically collects blood-sugar readings from a glucose meter and wirelessly transmits them to a secure Web site accessible to patients and their caregivers. Algorithms are applied to help identify trends.

Nurses are available for one-on-one coaching, and a variety of written diet and exercise regimens are available. Patients who achieve and maintain diabetes management goals—picking up their prescriptions, getting their blood tested— automatically receive discounts on Amazon.com. The rewards program reflects the belief that positive reinforcement is the best motivator.

Programs like inTouch are serious game-changers. "It's more efficient for the physicians," Pegus explained. "When they see a patient, they can see exactly what's been happening instead of starting from scratch. It's more efficient for the nurses because they can work with more patients in a given period of time. It also makes their encounters with patients more productive and satisfying because they know what the patient has been doing or has failed to do.

"We believe that a system like ours," Pegus added, "allows you to see a better clinical outcome and a better utilization of health care resources, because people will be going to the emergency room less and being hospitalized less."

Perhaps Pegus's most important contribution, however, will be her effect on the process of disease management care itself. The patient information she and SymCare are gathering and analyzing will provide the first statistically rigorous evaluation of this type of care. Caregivers and chronic patients alike need to know what is and isn't working, so that the process can be reengineered for prime performance.

▶ *Manage the continuum of care.*

Debra Geihsler grew up on 2,000 acres in Nebraska, where her parents grew wheat and cattle. At age 10 she was operating a tractor, and soon thereafter she was earning money by taming wild horses. Except for the occasional bumps and bruises Geihsler suffered from getting thrown, she had little interest in the practice of medicine. The patience she acquired breaking horses, however, has come in handy over her 25-plus years as an innovative, hard-driving health care executive.

For much of that time, Geihsler has been struggling to change the system. As a nation, she jokes, "We've created a beautiful health care system. We've just forgotten two parties—those who pay for it, the employers, and those who are supposed to be cared for, the patients. Otherwise it's great."

Most proposals, she says, are about repairing perceived problems—the conventional wisdom, for example, that we need more primary care doctors. "Actually, we don't," she told us. If health care were focused on preventing illness instead of treating it, we would have plenty of primary caregivers.

Geihsler's reengineering efforts have mainly involved process, specifically, where the work is being done—something that is every bit as important in optimizing processes as what is done and who does it. One of her major accomplishments has been to move physicians out of hospitals and offices and into the workplaces of potential patients.

Geihsler's journey from bronco buster to increasingly responsible positions at three health care delivery systems—vice president of Mercy Health System in Janesville, Wisconsin, president of the Advocate Medical Group in Chicago, and then CEO of Atrius Health in Boston—has taken many a turn. Her latest move is to Activate Healthcare in Indianapolis.

In 1985, Geihsler became the vice president of administrative services at Mercy Hospital in Port Huron, Michigan, and seven years later, she was named vice president of medical management and operations at the Mercy Health System in Janesville. "That was where I got my grounding," she says, "approaching health care delivery with a more streamlined, process-oriented, efficiency mind-set." To Geihsler, that meant delivering care in a doctor's office instead of a hospital.

Opting to bypass hospital-centric systems, she set about creating doctor-based ones, eventually managing physician groups of 300 or more in Midwestern cities. That meant reinventing the relationship between hospitals and doctors, a task that caught her interest because of its potential to drastically reduce hospitalizations. If more care is given on an outpatient basis, she says, it stands to reason that the rate of hospitalizations will come down.

Geihsler wanted the physicians she managed to become the major health care providers in their areas, responsible for treating most illnesses, practicing preventive medicine, and working collaboratively with specialists. Her doctors liked the idea but wanted extra training to handle the assignment. She arranged it.

Mercy built physician centers that provided every kind of service short of in-patient hospitalization. Financially speaking, they were enormously successful, Geihsler told us, "because with the primary care people and surgeons and lab and

radiology and surgery center all together, they could
all use the same staff support." But the benefits went
far beyond dollars: "We could track the continuum,
from patient entry point to outpatient surgery to
patient back out again, connecting all the points and
providing fabulous care."

At Advocate Medical Group, she took on a practice
facing multiple challenges. A surplus of primary
care physicians in Chicago meant that a newly
hired physician would struggle for at least two years
before he or she could build a financially successful
practice. And if the economy happened to slow,
so did the practice. Some patients went without
medical care while others depended on hospital
emergency rooms.

Geihsler had hoped to get patients to be more
proactive about health care. So she switched gears,
figuring out ways to get her physicians out into the
community where they could attract patients. It
was time to rethink process guidelines, especially
the conventional wisdom that doctors should stay
in their offices and refuse to make house calls.
That's when Geihsler found the Chicago Police
Department.

The policemen's union had been agitating for better
benefits for its members, giving Geihsler the opening

she needed. In short order, Advocate doctors began visiting police stations to interview and perform health-risk assessments. They took the officers' histories, noted their eating and drinking habits, and counseled them about lifestyle and hereditary illnesses. Next, they developed worksheets that outlined a series of actions to improve the officers' diets and exercise regimens, and appointments for physical exams were scheduled.

The program was a big hit with the officers, Geihsler told us. They loved the convenience of stationhouse exams, lining up out the door whenever doctors' visits were scheduled. Within a month, 10 percent of the officers interviewed had made, and kept, doctors' appointments.

"At first, some of the doctors had their doubts" about the stationhouse visits, Geihsler said. "They thought it was just going to add to their workload." But as it turned out, the doctors liked doing the assessments because they could manage the patients' care more knowledgeably and efficiently.

The idea for moving the health care process into the workplace grew in part from Geihsler's earlier experience starting free clinics for people of limited means. People simply wouldn't come in, she said. Worried about paying their bills, they were working two or three jobs while also taking care of children and elderly parents. Geihsler understood that behavior. "All of my family are either farmers or poor hourly workers of some kind," she told us. "I'm the only one who has health insurance. If I said to my sister—who has at least two jobs—how about getting a checkup? she'd say, 'Great. When do I fit that in?'"

It's not that people have no interest in their health. They think and talk about it all the time. But for millions of Americans, healthy behavior and doctors' appointments take more time and money than they can spare. The best way to reach them and convince them otherwise, Geihsler believes, is through their employers, the people who are paying for workers' health care already. "Why wouldn't they welcome a preventative program that improves employee health and cuts the employer's health care costs?"

By the time Geihsler left Advocate, the medical group was solidly in the black, exceeding budget expectations for more than six years. She attributes that to tight management by people who knew how to build physician group practices and were allowed to operate independently of a hospital.

Geihsler continued her innovative ways when she moved to Boston in 2006 to become the CEO of another challenged group practice, HealthOne, which was reorganized as Atrius Health, the parent of Harvard Vanguard Medical Associates.

Geihsler told us that she has always been bothered by the failure of typical medical practices to intervene with chronically ill patients. Take a patient with hypertension who has seen a doctor four times, say, over two years, always complaining of the same symptoms. Four times he has been told to stop using salt and start exercising. "We should be reaching out to those patients between visits," she says, "to get them to behave better so they won't have a stroke."

Even patients who normally follow a healthy regimen can stop eating properly and exercising regularly if a traumatic event occurs—a death or divorce, for example. Geihsler reengineered the processes in Atrius's primary-care clinics to create what she calls "in-between coaches," medical advisers who periodically contact these patients to get them back on the straight and narrow.

When she left Atrius in 2008, Geihsler launched a start-up, Activate Healthcare. The Indianapolis venture is embracing Geihsler's on-site health care model to reduce employers' insurance outlays. The company's mission: "Enabling employees to take charge of their health and employers to take charge of health care costs." Again, that means moving doctors out of their offices and into the places where patients spend their working hours.

"We found that, in any given corporation, 30 to 70 percent of these folks do not have an attachment to a primary care physician," Geihsler said. When asked, they may claim to have a regular doctor, she continued, but upon further questioning, a significant share will admit that they haven't seen that doctor for years.

> *"We found that, in any given corporation, 30 to 70 percent of these folks do not have an attachment to a primary care physician."*

The Activate model dictates that a physician and health coach spend an hour with each employee in the client company's offices, doing a physical exam, creating an action plan that pinpoints existing or potential problems, and laying out the behaviors the employee needs to adopt. Health coaches regularly connect with the employees to help keep them on track.

Convincing employees to eat food appropriate for their health conditions is always a challenge. Activate is exploring a variety of options—among them, enlisting restaurants to deliver healthy food to offices if the employees want it. That eliminates the danger of employees leaving the office for lunch and giving in to their unhealthy appetite for fast food or other poor choices. Activate also helps employers build benefit plans that encourage healthy behavior.

In promoting the on-site model, Geihsler describes a typical medical experience: You have a sore throat, an earache, a urinary tract infection, or some other common ailment. You call your doctor to ask what you should do, and the nurse insists you come in to see the doctor. You've got a busy schedule or a tight budget or both, so you wait two or three days, and eventually your problem seems to subside. Whether it has solved itself or gone into hiding to reappear at a later date is unknown. In any event, you've been suffering—needlessly, in Geihsler's opinion.

She insists there's a better way. The on-site physician does a thorough intake interview and checkup of new patients, including their physical and emotional states, family histories, and lifestyles. Health coaches maintain regular contact with patients to update their records and track their progress in achieving their action plan goals. Now, when a patient calls with a sore throat, the doctor can knowledgeably get on the phone and prescribe a solution, confident that the on-site nurse or nurse-practitioner will be there to monitor the situation.

In fact, Geihsler expects that physicians following
her model will one day dedicate the hours of 7:00
to 9:00 A.M. to answering e-mail or phone calls from
patients. With up-to-date information about each
patient at doctors' fingertips, and with the assurance
that trained aides are available at work sites, they
can quickly and easily make the right decisions and
provide immediate relief to patients suffering from
coughs, congestion, contact dermatitis, and the like
that uncomfortably strike all of us with regularity.

The greater goal, Geihsler reminds, is to improve the
quality of health care delivery—not just the quality
of the treatment patients receive for an injury or a
disease, but the quality of their health all through
their lives. And she believes her model can do that by
changing the way doctors do their work and interact
with their patients. "It's not just about how I treated
you once you became a diabetic," she insists, "but
whether I could have prevented you from becoming
a diabetic but didn't."

▶ *Leverage the physician's time.*

A veteran specializing in cardiology and internal
medicine at one of Harvard Vanguard's sites was
presiding over a shared medical appointment. In a
shared appointment, up to a dozen patients—some
with relatives in tow—see the same doctor at the
same time. This innovation is one of the process

reforms that Zeev Neuwirth believes will improve access to health care and raise the effectiveness of its delivery while also making the doctor's increasingly complex job more doable.

It was perhaps predictable that not all of Neuwirth's physician colleagues would be delighted with group patient visits. Would patients be candid in a group setting? Would they resent the loss of privacy? Could a doctor probe into each patient's personal problems or deliver bad news in a group setting?

The patients sat in a semicircle on chairs in the big conference room. The physician was assisted by a nurse, a documenter to enter his observations in each patient's medical record, and a facilitator to keep the visit process moving along. A longtime patient—we'll call him Bob—was reporting on his latest symptoms when he suddenly announced, "You know, I think I'm depressed, and I need some help with it."

After the session, the doctor buttonholed a colleague. "For years," he said, "I've been telling Bob he was depressed, and he wouldn't believe me. Now, in his first group visit, he stands up and acknowledges it. I almost fell off my chair!"

Bob's sudden self-realization, Neuwirth told us later, was not all that uncommon at group visits. "When people go for a one-on-one appointment," he said, "they often don't get to report new problems or get the information they need. Maybe they recognize that the doctor is pressured by time constraints, or maybe they just forget to ask. Many patients also feel isolated and vulnerable—being sick or having a chronic disease can be a very lonely thing." Group visits, he explained, have a kind of social network ambience. Patients feel freer to share their symptoms and their treatments and to learn from the experiences of others.

Bob's epiphany was testimony to the effectiveness of shared appointments, but the added efficiency they provide is just as valuable. By breaking down the doctor's work in patient visits and assigning others to keep a record, elicit questions, and facilitate the discussion, the group visit lets the doctor focus on what he or she does best. It also allows the doctor to process patients in parallel rather than singly, radically increasing the bandwidth of a process that had been linear. The cardiologist's 90-minute session with a dozen patients would have taken three hours if each had been given just 15 minutes, one-on-one.

And because they are both efficient and effective, group patient visits are slowly but steadily working their way into the practice of medicine. According to the American Academy of Family Physicians,

8.4 percent of doctors offered patients that option in 2008, up from 5.7 percent in 2005. At Harvard Vanguard, nearly 40 group visits run on a regular basis in specialties ranging from internal medicine to dermatology to ophthalmology, with dozens more planned.

The group approach was initially designed to give patients access to their doctors without the usual days or weeks of waiting, while also making far more efficient use of the doctor's time. But research suggests that the shared events can actually inspire better compliance. In some studies, for example, diabetics enrolled in shared appointments had lower blood sugar levels than comparably ill patients who saw their doctors singularly.

The group visits appear to be highly popular with patients. In a 2008 survey of 720 people who signed up for shared appointments at Harvard Vanguard, 77 percent said they would schedule another, while only 5 percent said they would not. Seventy-three percent thought their relationships with their doctors had improved as a result of shared appointments.

At the start of a typical group follow-up visit, before the doctor enters the room, the facilitator gets all the patients to sign an agreement saying they won't divulge what others say during the visit. Meanwhile, a nurse checks patients' vital signs and provides medication refills as needed. The facilitator has also written patients' names and the reasons for their visit on a whiteboard. Displayed on a second whiteboard, or easily accessible on a computer, is all the information the physician needs about each patient's medical history.

The doctor takes a history and does a brief physical examination based upon each patient's symptoms, announcing issues and conclusions so that they can be entered by the documenter in the patient's medical record. If the symptoms or problems require the patient to undress for a more thorough physical exam, it's done behind a curtain. The doctor delivers a diagnosis and treatment plan based on his or her findings, answers the patient's questions, and moves on to the next person.

After completing a patient's history and physical exam, the physician checks over the documenter's entries to make sure all questions have been answered and no problem overlooked. While the doctor is checking any previous notes with the documenter, the facilitator is starting a discussion among the patients. After Bob announced his depression, for example, the facilitator asked, "Who else has had problems with sadness or depression? Let's talk about it." One and then another patient would typically have spoken up, describing symptoms and treatments before the facilitator steered the talk to the next topic.

At some point, the doctor might have weighed in with suggestions regarding depression. But what the patients find most rewarding about group visits, according to Neuwirth, is not only the doctor's contribution but the discussion itself—the sharing of patient knowledge and experience.

Some patient visits are particularly suited to group treatment. Post-operative sessions with surgeons, for instance, are often devoted to repetitive lectures. In a shared medical appointment, a surgeon can quickly check out the post-op conditions of a dozen rotator-cuff patients, let's say, answer their questions, and deliver the standard lecture only once. Then the patients can trade experiences with others in the shared-recovery process.

As Neuwirth put it to us: "Think about how many times a physician says the same thing over and over each week to patients in individual visits. There are mini-lectures about blood pressure, diet, headache, back pain, medication side effects, pre- and post-operative instructions. If the physician were able to say all of it to a dozen patients at once, think how much time would be saved. Instead of the one-minute sound bite of information, a doctor could take a few minutes to really teach patients—and really listen to what's going on with them. Also, patients would have a chance to ask questions of one another and to support each other."

Even when they understand the benefits, though, not all physicians are enamored of the shared appointment model. Some say they don't want to give up the kind of intimate, knowledgeable connections they have with their longtime patients. But Neuwirth believes the group experience is inherently preferable. "People want to share their medical problems, and they want to hear about other people's medical problems," he says. "Health care should be a communal activity; the development of the individual visit in the ambulatory care setting was a medical establishment misstep. Doing surgery one patient at a time makes sense. Using the same model for chronic disease and preventative primary care doesn't."

Part of the patients' preference for group visits, Neuwirth told us, derives from an almost prurient curiosity about other people's problems. At the same time, patients genuinely empathize with others, and in shared appointments they constantly "step up and help each other," he said.

Neuwirth cautions that doctors and their teams need some training to make shared sessions successful. "Most physicians and staff are not competent in this kind of experience," he remarked. The facilitator, documenter, and medical assistant must be trained for their tasks along with the doctor. With the right training and setting, patients can have the kind of relaxed, in-depth experience that's difficult to find nowadays in a single-patient appointment. As for the physicians, Neuwirth declared, "It takes them back to the reason they went into medicine in the first place—to focus on their patients and to provide relationship-based medical care."

A CHECKLIST FOR PROCESS

▶ Have you identified the processes for which reengineering can make a significant improvement in efficiency and quality? In the final chapter of this book, we will tell you more about how to focus your reengineering efforts, but be sure that you have chosen areas that will produce important changes. Although we have told you to "start small", your results should still be significant. Your target processes and results must be compelling for clinicians to take notice.

▶ Can you demonstrate results quickly enough to maintain momentum? It's important for people engaged in reengineering to experience successful work change quickly. The faster they experience the benefits of work change, the faster they will become engaged. Early indicators of success also tell you that you are headed in the right direction.

▶ In setting the objectives for process change, have you gone far enough to address the systemic issues that are driving inefficiency and endangering safety? It may look easier to accomplish incremental change, but unless you go far enough, you may just be covering up problems—not really making the workplace better.

▶ Have you selected a reengineering leader who has the respect of other clinicians? We will talk more about this in the next chapter dealing with people, but health care professionals can only be led by those whose knowledge and character they highly respect.

▶ Do you have the support of the executive team of your enterprise? The details of health care-delivery change will come from the bottom up, but top-down engagement and support is also critical to accomplish major change. If you don't have support from the top, you will be limited in what you can do. We offer some advice in the pages ahead on how to get the support you need.

▶ Are you focused on processes populated with knowledgeable and engaged people? Go to where you have expertise and at least one catalyst to begin the change.

▶ Have you prepared for a long reengineering journey? Although we emphasize focus and starting in small venues where you can be successful, your reengineering will be a journey, not a single event. The more you experience the success of change, the more your appetite for change will grow—especially in the delivery of care where so much needs doing. If you pace change correctly, you will not be left exhausted, and the exhilaration of success will keep you going.

▶ Does your process redesign address the fragmentation of health care? One of the objectives of reengineering should be to address a continuum of care that can be managed by both the physician and the patient. Care will be delivered in multiple places—physicians' offices, clinics, hospitals, the workplace, and in patients' homes—and all will need to be elegantly connected.

► Will your process improvement lead to a more knowledgeable and engaged patient, able to make more intelligent decisions? What the patient hears and learns is critical. Education must be built into delivery processes. It cannot be an afterthought.

► When you are done, will you have significantly improved the lives of physicians, patients, and staff? Of course, dramatically improved clinical outcomes should be the objective of your reengineering, but your success will also be measured by how both patients and physicians experience the change in the quality of their lives.

We have only begun to describe the myriad medical processes that will have to be transformed in the reengineering of health care delivery. From birth to death, most of us will experience hundreds, maybe thousands of processes in hospitals, clinics, and doctors' offices, not to mention those in schools, corporate offices, pharmacies, ambulances, and medevac choppers, or at accident sites and on ski vacations. The venues are endless—and all can be improved. What counts, as we have stressed in this chapter, is how process changes will be made and the need for open-mindedness as the people entrusted with health care reengineering risk new approaches.

All of us who are involved with health care, not just those at the top, must be ready to embrace change while learning to operate in a transformed world. That's the subject of the next chapter.

CHAPTER 5

REMEMBER PEOPLE

The eminently quotable George Bernard Shaw noted that "the people who get on in this world are the people who get up and look for the circumstances they want, and if they can't find them, make them."

It's clear that the reengineering of health care must take advantage of rapidly evolving new technology, and the processes for delivering health care must be transformed as well. But neither of these changes can happen without attention to the human side of the equation. After all, health care is often intensely personal, intimate, and emotional. The skills and behavior of the people who deliver health care are crucial to any reform.

Physicians, in particular, are likely to view the transformation as especially difficult. For them, the issue isn't one of skills or professional knowledge; most physicians admirably measure up on both scores. Nor do they lack the desire to improve health care. But as individualists trained to be the mainsprings of their practices, they tend to lack team-building skills and usually don't believe that improvement requires any real change in the way they do their work and relate to their patients and associates. In addition, most have spent the majority of their adult lives practicing medicine, and have not been exposed to management methods employed in other industries. Either way, they are wrong, of course, and their behavior must change, because without the active participation of physicians, health care delivery cannot be successfully reengineered.

Changing someone's behavior is never easy. But there are people working in health care right now who are getting up and making the circumstances they want by leading their colleagues to a more efficient and effective future.

Changing someone's behavior is never easy. But there are people working in health care right now who are getting up and making the circumstances they want by leading their colleagues to a more efficient and effective future. The lessons gleaned from the experiences of these reformers are not only valuable, but replicable. Here's how you can follow their lead:

▶ *Inspire your people with others' success.*

When Zeev Neuwirth began his reengineering initiative at Harvard Vanguard Medical Associates, he quietly introduced his reforms only to the internal medicine practice. He didn't want to have to deal with a practice full of skeptical doctors and managers as well as with enterprise-level process and technology problems. Then he was named Vice President of Clinical Effectiveness and Innovation,

with an open mandate to make changes. That's
when he realized he couldn't get anywhere without
the enthusiastic support of the group practice's top
people, both administrative and clinical.

To win them over, he held up the astonishing results
of a restructuring at a health care organization
similar to Harvard Vanguard. It took a good deal
of persuasion, but Neuwirth convinced four of the
Massachusetts practice's senior chiefs to give up
three days of work to travel with him to Appleton,
Wisconsin. That's how Harvard Vanguard's chiefs of
surgery, internal medicine, operations, and finance
came to visit ThedaCare, whose 5,000 employees are
spread among four hospitals, a physicians' group,
and a variety of community health services.

The chiefs were skeptical, to say the least, and
Neuwirth had a lot riding on the visit. "I couldn't
sleep the night before we left Boston," he told us. "I
thought, if this doesn't work, if they don't see how
important this is and that it's possible to make these
changes happen, the game's over."

Within a few minutes of arriving at ThedaCare, the
visitors met a vice president of clinical operations
who asked what Harvard Vanguard was working on.
The chief of surgical services at Harvard Vanguard,

who was standing next to Neuwirth, mentioned a newly begun redesign project in orthopedics, where the goal was to improve productivity by 25 percent. "That's great," the ThedaCare VP responded. "We just did a similar orthopedics project and improved productivity by 400 percent." He proceeded to describe—"simply and elegantly, and with disarming humility," Neuwirth recalls—how the miracle was accomplished. The Harvard Vanguard chief turned to Neuwirth and said, "If we don't learn anything else in the next couple of days, what I just heard would make it worth the trip."

Later in the visit, Harvard Vanguard's CFO became a bit skeptical, demanding that then-CEO Dr. John Toussaint divulge ThedaCare's financial profile. "I want to know the bottom line here," the CFO said, "how much money have you spent on this reengineering effort and how much money have you recouped?"

Toussaint replied that he had assigned his own CFO to keep track of those numbers over the two years it took to complete the initial redesign project. In the first year, it turned out that $2 million was spent and $12 million was recouped, and the next year's results were identical. Then, Toussaint continued, he informed his CFO (perhaps mischievously) that the finance department was next in line for reengineering. The result was another few million dollars of overhead chopped from the finance department's own operations.

Neuwirth, his portable video camera running, caught the stunned but impressed Harvard Vanguard CFO simply nodding his head.

▶ *Change skills and, sometimes, change people.*

It's no secret that elderly patients have trouble with medications. In a recent study of people 57 to 85 years old, a University of Chicago team found that half the people it surveyed were taking five prescribed pills a day, plus dietary supplements. Nationwide, at least 2 million people in that age group are believed to be ingesting a potentially risky mix of medications. Serious problems can arise if they forget or don't hear all of the doctor's instructions for taking the drugs, or if they take the pills too often or skip a dose.

In 2005, Novant Health, a large, North Carolina-based nonprofit hospital system, quantified the problem. After being discharged, patients 65 and over were twice as likely as other patients to be treated in the emergency room for an adverse drug event (ADE), and they were seven times as likely to be readmitted.

The pharmacist—whose vital role in health care has long been recognized—holds the solution. In ancient times, Japan's pharmacists and their assistants were revered; in fact, the imperial household's pharmacist outranked the emperor's two personal physicians. And in the United States today, our neighborhood pharmacists can and may provide a critical safeguard for elderly customers.

As ordered by the Medicare Part D prescription-drug program, the pharmacist's computer lists all drugs an elderly person is taking and flags potentially dangerous interactions when the patient uses the same pharmacy consistently. Pharmacists also may repeat the instructions and give advice to their customers, such as, "Take this before you go to bed," or "Don't take this pill on an empty stomach."

But hospital pharmacists are different. Most work behind the scenes with little direct contact to either the hospital's patients or the prescribing doctors. The Novant report told how changes could be made, and how health care workers could collaborate and work together to improve the patient experience with prescription-drug issues.

Novant understood that older patients were not purposely overdosing or ignoring doctors' instructions. Rather, the hospital efforts to educate

patients about their medications often were
forgotten or confused once the patient returned
home. But the problem was a tricky one. To begin
with, the hospital pharmacists and hospital
physicians were not aware what drugs patients
already had in their medicine cabinets at home.
Exacerbating the problem was the fact that some
hospital patients came in without a supply of
their usual medications and were then given new
prescriptions. When they came home and found
the old pills, some took both the old and new
prescriptions, risking an overdose. A better discharge
process, with people trained to work with patients
after discharge, when they returned home, was one
solution.

In 2006, Novant reengineered its pioneering
disease-management program, strengthening
the discharge process at its 12 hospitals to better
focus on the needs of elderly patients. Instead of
simply sending people home with the usual written
instructions and prescriptions, Novant added two
crucial checkpoints through its Safe Med patient
outreach program. Pharmacists were trained to
follow up by calling older patients at home after
their discharge. They double-checked the patients'
prescriptions, including the medications previously
in the home, and instructed them about proper
dosages, side effects, and negative drug interactions.

The pharmacists also left phone numbers where they could be reached and urged the patients, or family members, to call back with any questions. Information gathered in the calls was entered into electronic health care database and shared with their physicians, providing both patient and doctor with a reconciled list of the patient's medications.

Nan Holland is Novant's senior director of clinical excellence and was there at Safe Med's inception, told us that the innovative program came very close to failing.

Novant's doctors backed the program in the new-idea stage, and corporate approval and funding were secured. But after Safe Med was plugged in for a trial run at one hospital, the planners discovered two major issues. The first problem arose, Holland recalled, because the plan failed to understand the importance of hiring "five pharmacists who had the right skill set and relationship to talk with patients." The pharmacists initially selected were not accustomed to working directly with patients and counseling them about their meds. They preferred to work in the doctors' offices and see the patients during and following the office visit—a process the doctors and patients found intrusive and distracting. "Our doctors became frustrated," Holland told us, "and said, 'I just don't understand what we're trying to accomplish here.' They wanted the help, but the model did not work."

Initially there was an attempt to interact with patients at the point of hospital discharge—just when patients were being released. "The main thing on patients' minds the day of discharge," Holland said, "is getting out of the hospital. They really aren't a receptive audience and it was not a good time to engage the patient." Building any kind of relationship or properly instructing patients about their medications was out of the question.

Holland and her team found solutions to both problems. They redesigned the patient-education process, opting for telephone interviews once the patients arrived home, and they hired pharmacists who had experience dealing directly with patients. Soon, all 12 of Novant's hospitals adopted the Safe Med program.

Each week, the pharmacists receive a list of high-risk older patients discharged from Novant's hospitals. They examine the patients' discharge records, looking for signs of existing or potential drug-related issues. They also targeted four types of drugs frequently involved in adverse drug events—anticoagulants (blood thinners), hypoglycemics, sedatives, and digoxin (used to treat heart conditions).

The pharmacists, using templates developed by Novant Safe Med and Disease Management teams to guide them, then make their calls. They spend the first few minutes making patients feel comfortable with the process, after which they ask them to gather all their medications and read off the labels to the pharmacist. The aim is to make certain a patient's supply of drugs matches the patient's discharge medications list. The reading also discloses what over-the-counter medications and supplements or medications from another physician a patient may be using. Once a patient's drugs have been identified, the pharmacist explains the purpose and proper usage of each one, including possible negative effects and interactions with other drugs.

Terri Cardwell, pharmacist and manager of the program, reports that in the course of the discussion, a patient will often raise issues or concerns they may not have previously discussed with a doctor, which can have a profound impact on recovery.

When the conversation is over, the pharmacists enter the medication assessment and what they have learned into Novant's electronic Disease Management records system. The entry also includes the pharmacist's assessment of the patient and suggestions for possible changes in medications. This material is also sent directly to the patient's physician. The whole process, including preparation, conversation, and wrap-up, takes one hour on average.

The pharmacist's expanded role triggered complaints from some of Novant's physicians. "There was initially some concern about giving my patient information when I'm not there, or about the pharmacists expanding their scope of practice," Holland told us. But that problem was settled by discussing all issues with the physician steering committee, which has to approve each phase of the disease-management programs. At first, Holland said, the committee's members were not completely engaged in the reengineering concept itself, but now "it's a very dynamic group. Many evenings we practically have to run out of the room when the meeting is over because they offer a lot of input and are very engaged in helping to build these programs and enjoy the collaboration."

Safe Med has demonstrated its value many times over. By building a bridge between patients and their health care providers, the project has improved the lives of patients and dramatically lowered ADE-related readmission rates. The patients who participate in the program have expressed gratitude for the pharmacist who have provided them with information and tools to improve their medication use. This has also resulted in a decrease chance of having a drug reaction and returning to the emergency department or hospital. Adverse drug-related admissions have plummeted from 17.9 percent of total admissions to 4 percent.

The project has also demonstrated how pharmacists can be an active part of the health care team and can add more value to health care delivery. Safe Med received the 2008 award of the American Society of Health-System Pharmacists (ASHP) for excellence in medication-use safety. At the awards event, a speaker hailed the Safe Med Team, saying, "You've probably done more for our profession with this program than all of us have done in a long time." If the rhetoric sounds as if some virulent epidemic has been stamped out, we are not quite there yet, but the focus and attention to medication management is indeed making an impact on patient safety—and an indication of what reengineering could do for people everywhere.

▶ *Employ the skills of your nurses.*

We were close to the end of our interview with Maggie Lohnes, clinical information management administrator at the four-hospital MultiCare Health system based in Tacoma, Washington. We had listened as she told us how she had started her medical career in California as a registered nurse, served eight years in intensive care, and then became fascinated by information technology.

"This is my passion," she said. "I wanted to be a nurse when I was 10. When I made a decision to stop taking care of patients directly, it was a hard decision. It became my way of giving care."

Lohnes told us of the initiatives she had devised to win the support of clinicians for MultiCare's electronic health-record project. And then we asked her a question that had nagged us for some time: Why is it that many of the leaders of reengineering efforts we met around the country were nurses, not physicians?

> *Why is it that many of the leaders of reengineering efforts we met around the country were nurses, not physicians?*

"We're just really smart," she joked, before turning serious. "Nurses are taught to pay parallel attention to the patient's body systems and the monitoring systems," she told us. "We're trained to trust in our knowledge and react appropriately when necessary—and remain calm throughout that process. Nurses and physicians are a lot alike in that, of course, but physicians get to yell."

It struck us that the person she was describing is a systems thinker, in close and intimate connection with each health care process, who also has a strong emotional investment in the well-being of the patients under his or her care. And a nurse, with less power and ego than doctors enjoy, is also more apt to be flexible and open to change. That combination creates a powerful capacity to lead the kind of transformative work we describe in this book.

The lesson: In planning and implementing any kind of health care reengineering project, be sure not to ignore the valuable and insightful potential contributions of the nursing corps.

▶ *Enlist the eager young leaders.*

When Zeev Neuwirth began to reengineer the delivery of health care at Harvard Vanguard Medical Associates in Boston, he was aiming much higher than the usual short-lived quality campaigns that many hospitals and medical practices periodically order up. Typically, these drives come with a blizzard of speeches, e-mails, and meetings meant to whip up enthusiasm and activity. Here and there, some numbers will move temporarily—and success will be proclaimed. For Neuwirth, that would be a baby step. "We need to establish an accountability infrastructure," he said—in effect, a whole new culture that would spur all of his group practice's doctors, other clinicians, and staff members to change how they do things and adapt to profound new ways of delivering health care.

As related earlier, Neuwirth had won the backing of the group's top brass. But he was convinced that if the program were to succeed, the practice's frontline clinical and administrative leaders would have to show the way. "No matter how good your central institutional leadership," he says, "health care progress happens at the practice level, and I've never seen or heard of any breakthrough without a local frontline clinical leader having taken a step beyond."

> *Health care progress happens at the practice level, and I've never seen or heard of any breakthrough without a local frontline clinical leader having taken a step beyond.*

At Harvard Vanguard, that should not have been a problem. The practice was loaded with top-notch people, some of the best doctors in the country. Who better to lead their colleagues toward change?

But some of the senior physicians balked, for an understandable reason. Clinicians are not trained as team leaders, performance managers, or communicators. Leading transformational change is not taught in medical schools, residencies, or fellowships. Many of the established doctors and department chiefs at Harvard Vanguard had trouble envisioning how things might change. Offered a chance to try something new, their response was: "Thanks, but no thanks."

As Chief of Clinical Effectiveness and Innovation at Harvard Vanguard, Neuwirth could have insisted. Instead, he decided to work around the senior staff's disinterest by beginning with the practice's future leaders, where there was some enthusiasm and energy. He chose 20 people from the rising generation of clinicians and used them as the nucleus of a new Leadership Academy in transformative reengineering. Eager to advance and not yet set in their ways, the younger doctors were excited by the opportunity Neuwirth was proposing.

The future leaders met only two hours a month at the beginning of the program—"I like to start really small with this kind of stuff," Neuwirth told us. Even so, the response was amazing, both from the participants themselves and from the nurses and administrators across the practice who dealt with the young doctors.

Attitudes were noticeably changing for the better,
and cooperation and efficiency were thriving.
The buzz was so positive that, within three or four
months, the department chiefs were asking to be
included. That's when Neuwirth happily expanded
the program to accommodate his new converts.

He conducted interviews and meetings to determine
the immediate needs of the physician leaders as
they went through their day. He designed an 80-hour
curriculum and brought in outside experts to help
teach such skills as setting goals, assessing processes,
planning change, managing performance, and
estimating costs and benefits. But this was not like an
MBA program. What counted more than the content
was what happened after the classes ended and the
students began applying what they had learned.

Typically, Neuwirth says, physicians who are
assigned operational and administrative functions
have a tendency to plateau relatively fast. "They
learn some new things in the first few months," he
says, "then learning stops, sometimes for years.
Dozens of doctors have told me that in the first six
months or year of their administrative roles, they
experienced great personal development. But they
haven't learned much in the past 15 years of being a
chief. They may have attended a leadership course or
seminar once or twice, but that's it."

"This is sad and dangerous," Neuwirth went on. "It's a recipe for stagnation and status quo. Perhaps, one of the reasons health care delivery isn't changing as fast as it should is because we haven't created a community of learner-leaders."

The Leadership Academy reawaken*s* Neuwirth's converts to the joys of their profession, he told us. Suddenly, they are growing and developing again— reading articles, experimenting, discussing new ideas with colleagues, and networking with people in other specialties and departments. Participation in the academy, he says, is a life-altering experience that can only advance the practice of medicine, both operationally and clinically.

The last session of Neuwirth's expanded program brought another payoff. For nine months, 35 men and women—primarily doctors, but some nurses and administrators, as well—had been meeting once a month for intense four- to six-hour sessions. For most of them, what they had learned, and their experience in implementing their new knowledge, had transformed their work and their lives. They had begun to form clinical teams in which all parties—medical assistants, nurses, secretaries, and physicians—treat each other with respect and work every day to examine and improve their delivery of health care. They had become the missionaries for reengineering the Harvard Vanguard practice.

"People had tears in their eyes during the last seminar. They were so moved by what they had experienced over the past nine months," Neuwirth told us. "In the give-and-take, they had become really close to each other. And for the chiefs who had reached a plateau in their careers, the program gave them back the feeling of growing and improving. They had a renewed sense of purpose and hope."

In the academy's opening sessions, Neuwirth delivers a message that resonates with the entire clinical practice. He reminds his colleagues of how the system, perhaps inadvertently, belittles doctors and diminishes their ability to effect change by labeling them "thought leaders," implying that they don't know how to get things done. "Aren't you sick and tired of being treated as smart little drones, highly skilled technicians doing someone else's bidding?" Then he challenges his students: "Don't you actually want to change health care? Well, here's your chance." The academy's defiant motto, a phrase Neuwirth thought up while driving to a Leadership Academy session, is: "We turn thought leaders into action leaders."

And action is built into the curriculum. From the very first session, Neuwirth tells his startled colleagues that he's not interested in how much they learn from the academy, and if their only goal is to learn, they should go get a graduate degree. His measure of their success—and the academy's primary purpose—is to create positive change in their departments, at their practice sites, and throughout Harvard Vanguard as a whole. Even before the first session, participants are asked to write down their specific goals for creating change. The goals are then typed up, inserted into their notebooks, and reviewed with the entire class.

Before the end of every class session, the students write down one or two things they are going to change in their practices as a result of what they have just learned. And at the beginning of every session, the class members spend the first 45 minutes reporting on the past month, the changes they tried to put into effect, the challenges they faced, what they learned, and the end result.

The impact of this action-oriented approach is widely evident at Harvard Vanguard. Over 150 doctors, nurses, and administrators from every practice site have participated in the Leadership Academy, "uniting and aligning the entire organization through a network of distributed leadership," Neuwirth told us. Over 80 percent of the participants have been promoted or assigned to a major strategic organizational initiative.

At a recent Obstetrics and Gynecology department
meeting, for example, the entire department came
together to uproot about 25 years of practice by
switching from one hospital to another. "That's the
type of thing people literally quit over," Neuwirth
told us. "But not one voice was raised and no one
disagreed with the overall direction at a three-hour
meeting of more than a hundred people. It was a
phenomenon to watch and a credit to Dr. Susan
Haas, the chief of the department, and the other
clinical leaders present," he said. It happened, in
part, because about a dozen of the people in the
department had been through Neuwirth's leadership
training program.

Before the big meeting, the chief brought the
leadership-trained physicians together and simply
said, "I need your help. You are all leaders. We're
all in this together and understand the challenges
of change and the importance of putting aside
differences in order to achieve the best patient
care possible. Here's the hill we have to climb." The
group responded by working out plausible ideas that
were presented to doctors, technicians, midwives,
administrators, and others at the meeting.

That kind of teamwork and applied leadership
in bringing new ideas in a fraught situation
is innovation in Neuwirth's estimation. "It's

person-to-person social marketing—more like grassroots community organizing than some spreadsheet approach to process redesign," he says, and it works to transform cultures and attract new talent. Indeed, the transformation of health care delivery at Harvard Vanguard, this "innovation culture," as Neuwirth told us, is becoming "the number one selling point" for the organization's physician recruiters.

Most of the Leadership Academy's efforts focus on the clinicians' interactions with the members of their staff. The doctors learn a new way of communicating, an approach that treats staffers as equals and seeks their help in improving the team's operations. There's no shame in failure. Making patient care better is obviously the goal," Neuwirth says, "but you have to try and fail and learn, and then try again with something different and better. That's the story of most successful people or groups."

The academy teaches a protocol for this collegial approach, including language that helps in creating new and better relationships. The phrase "yes, but" is discouraged, for example. When a staff member offers an opposing opinion, the academy students don't dismiss the alternative outright. Instead, they are taught to ask questions or say something like, "How would we build on what so-and-so said?"

Recently, to improve the academy's results, Neuwirth met with some former students and their colleagues. They included nurses, medical assistants, secretaries, administrators, and physicians. He heard the by-now-familiar stories of chiefs astounding the nurses and administrators with their dramatic behavioral changes and newfound leadership abilities. He also discovered that academy graduates were still practicing what they had been taught—and they were enjoying greater efficiency and stronger team relationships because of it.

Even more surprising and gratifying was Neuwirth's recent discovery that the same collaborative language and approach are still being used throughout the Kenmore Internal Medicine practice, where he introduced it nearly five years ago. It's a testament to the sustainability of what he has built at Harvard Vanguard.

In the course of the discussion, Neuwirth noticed that a particular phrase kept cropping up. He didn't comment at the time, but his delight was evident when he described the experience to us. "One person would say, 'I'd like to build on what Rebecca said,' and then a few minutes later, someone else would say the same thing. The technique I had taught them had become not just a part of their vocabulary, but also a part of their culture. It was embedded in the way they treat each other." He paused just a moment before adding, "No wonder they're getting such good results."

We believe that Zeev Neuwirth has it right: In health care as in other industries, breakthroughs come when leaders have the courage and good sense to abandon outmoded ways and begin to tap into the talent, aspirations, and ideas of a new generation. Had Neuwirth not turned to the future leaders at Harvard Vanguard when the senior staff rejected change, the reengineering of the group practice might have withered and died. Instead, he began an amazing transformation that shows the way for health care practitioners across the country.

In health care as in other industries, breakthroughs come when leaders have the courage and good sense to abandon outmoded ways and begin to tap into the talent, aspirations, hopes, and ideas of a new generation.

A CHECKLIST FOR THE PEOPLE SIDE

▶ Have you adjusted your operating style to address changes in social interactions between your staff? Reengineering health care delivery requires a social intervention to create mutual respect between team members.

▶ Have you documented issues of quality, safety, and inefficiency and have you found examples of how others have successfully addressed these issues? Clinicians require proof that new approaches to health care delivery will work. What's more, the safety of patients is at stake.

▶ Have you identified the clinicians who will lead your reengineering initiatives? Our research and our own experiences tell us that a clinician must lead any reengineering effort. The work of clinicians cannot be reengineered for them. It must be reengineered by them and with them.

▶ Have you engaged the missionaries in your organization who will encourage others to engage in changes? No single leader can accomplish the changes required in health care delivery. He or she needs the help of others who share an appetite for change, vision of the future, and inclination to get things done.

▶ Have you defined how the behaviors of people have to change? It's important to identify how behaviors contribute to issues to quality, safety, and inefficiency—and then to take actions that will change those behaviors.

▶ Do you have the right people on your reengineering teams? Do they have the substance (what they know) and style (how they operate) to accomplish change? Knowledge of the areas to be reengineered is critical. Too much is at stake to trust a superficial understanding of the field.

▶ Once a new process is in place, do you have the right people with the right skills in the jobs? Reengineering usually affords people the opportunity to demonstrate a broader range of their skills. But sometimes new people with different skills are required to do the job.

As the past three chapters have clearly shown, reengineering work must take into account the three core areas of new technology, transformed processes, and changes in the behavior of the people doing the work. For another example of how all three can be successfully meshed, the next chapter looks at the way Tom Knight reengineered health care—with a focus on quality and safety—at one of Houston's major delivery systems.

CHAPTER 6

MEET TOM KNIGHT, REENGINEER

When he's talking about the risks of health care, Dr. Tom Knight likes to recall the time he took his son and daughter to an adventure camp in Missouri. One of the challenges involved climbing a 30-foot-high pole to stand on a small platform and, then, the children leap into midair to catch hold of a stationary trapeze set about six feet away. The children are attached to a harness and belayed from the ground, but the jump was a true leap of faith.

It's just as scary to be in a hospital Knight contends. "We ask our patients to jump off faith poles every single day. Think about the faith it takes to have a nurse administer a medication—through an IV— that's going to be in your heart in 10 seconds. Is it the right medicine? Did she check? It's terrifying," as he well knows. His job, in a sound bite, is to roll out the safety net and make sure it holds. In this chapter, you'll see how Knight is leading that at Houston's sprawling Methodist Hospital System by redesigning the way health care is delivered.

Tom Knight is the Senior Vice President and Chief Quality Officer of the four-hospital complex (a fifth hospital is scheduled to open in November 2010). He has been obsessed his entire career with patient safety and the quality of care patients receive. His passion was apparent in earlier appointments at Forsyth Medical Group in Winston-Salem, North

Carolina, and the California Pacific Medical Center in San Francisco, as well as in leadership roles with professional organizations, such as the National Committee for Quality Assurance.

Now, health care quality, and therefore Knight's turn in the spotlight, has arrived.

Never before have these issues so consumed the agendas of hospitals across the nation, spurred on by consumer groups, the media, and especially the U.S. government. Medicare and Medicaid payments, for example, now rise or fall depending on hospitals' ability to reduce complications attributable to their procedures.

Yet, as Knight told us, the irony is that the seemingly simplest things are often the hardest to get right. Unwashed or improperly washed hands, for example, are notorious disease spreaders, both in and out of hospitals. But getting people to wash before and after they come in contact with a patient is an incredibly difficult thing to pull off, he said. But with more than 95 percent compliance rate, Houston Methodist can now claim success on the hand-washing front, but it didn't come easy.

"We went through a whole program that incorporated a lot of components," Knight said.

"But because hand washing is really a cultural or habitual thing, not something that technology can fix, the hospital's leaders had to model and inspire rather than manage."

And they did it in innovative ways, one of which Knight good-naturedly described as "putting some leadership skin in the game." Any senior leader caught not washing his or her hands properly or applying antibacterial gel after entering or leaving a patient-care area was liable to a fine on the spot. The culprit had to hand over a $20 bill.

Keeping track of patients' medications is another black hole in American hospital care. "You would think that with technology that can get a heart attack patient a complex angioplasty 47 minutes after he or she comes through the hospital door," Knight said, "we could figure out which medicines you're on when you come into the hospital and tell you accurately what to take when you leave. But that has proved to be the biggest challenge in American health care.

"It's the sheer volume, the average number of prescriptions that patients coming into the hospital take," he explained, "the number of prescribers and the lack of coordination in that arena. Then, when you're in the hospital, you end up interacting with a lot of different physicians, usually many times. So trying to get all of those on the same page, and to get everybody the right prescriptions, and at the same time go to a unified list—it's just a huge challenge."

Most of the safety- and quality-improvement efforts are being hindered by a serious lack of culture and infrastructure advancement. Knight graphically described the situation by calling to mind a photo that depicted health care as the Wright Brothers' plane, *The Flyer*, with a Boeing 747 engine sitting atop the flimsy little wood and fabric machine—the point being that the advances in diagnostic and treatment capabilities have outgrown the health care delivery infrastructure. That perception has led him to reengineer the way Methodist Hospital does business—and he's doing it just as we would advise, in terms of the three pillars of technology, process, and people.

> *Advances in diagnostic and treatment*
> *capabilities have outgrown the health care*
> *delivery infrastructure.*

"In the old days," he told us, "the quality-control people would measure, ask you to do a better job, and come back six months later to see how you were doing." Now, there is no such luxury of time.

As the quality officer, he must get directly involved
in the process to help people figure out how to do
it better. "My job today is to actually facilitate the
reengineering of the work processes … [that will be]
followed by the doctors and all the staff." The trick
is to incorporate the key changes smoothly into the
process of health care delivery. "We have to figure out
how to make the right thing to do, the easiest thing to
do," Knight says.

Methodist is one of America's largest private,
nonprofit medical complexes, serving more than
600,000 patients a year. It has a long heritage of
health care breakthroughs, including the world's first
multiple-organ transplant, and it consistently ranks
among the top institutions in *U.S. News & World
Report* listings. Yet, like most other leading medical
institutions, Methodist recognizes that major
reforms are essential.

The chief technical problem Methodist faced in
reengineering its processes, Knight told us, was
"too many moving parts—too many doctors and
nurses prescribing too many medicines for too
many patients. In addition, patients were confronted
with a massive and confusing bureaucracy that
required them to interact with some 27 clinicians
and staff members during a four-day stay in the
hospital. And the sheer complexity of coordinating

between 27 individuals taxed the hospital's ability to communicate with patients in a timely and forthright manner, not to mention that complexity is a Petri dish for error.

To alleviate the communication bottlenecks, the hospital worked to standardize patient procedures, paying particular attention to information about specific patients that heightened their risk profiles.

One process that Methodist targeted—the ordering of tests and treatments by physicians—illustrates the complexity of the reengineering task as a whole. As frequently happens, the redesign began with new technology.

For generations, speakers at medical conventions would ask their audiences to name the most important piece of medical equipment. The right answer was not some high-tech device like an MRI, but rather the lowly pen. A doctor's pen in hand, the speaker would point out, controlled everything about the patient's treatment. The doctor wrote his or her instructions on the order form in the patient's medical record and that was that.

That simple answer doesn't work today. The combination of bad handwriting on the part of medical practitioners, careless recordkeeping, and

extremely complicated equipment and treatment
procedures leads to dangerous mistakes. So Knight
and Methodist turned to computerized physician
order entry (commonly known as CPOE), a
technological innovation for organizing care.

The decision to go with a technological solution
was just the first step. CPOE eliminates many safety
issues like handwriting and transcription errors. It
also allows for automatic alerts for issues such as
exceeding recommended doses of medication or
drug interactions. However, it carries it's own risks.
It must be smoothly and safely incorporated into
the flow of care. The processes being computerized
had to be redesigned, physician support marshaled,
and extra safety measures put in place to keep
the care-giving system operating properly. A team
made up of physicians, nurses, pharmacists, other
caregivers, and senior management was assembled
to consider the various systems available and to
choose technology that could be integrated with
the hospital's existing procedures. They also had to
consider what kind of safeguards would be built into
the system without compromising timeliness. When
a doctor orders a test or treatment, how quickly it's
delivered is often crucial to a patient's outcome.
Finally, the team had to select a vendor that could
deliver its prescriptions.

The journey is well on its way but will take another year and a half to complete. At Methodist today, all orders for medications must be entered into the hospital's central database. Two massive robots in the basement put a bar code on every dose of medication given a patient.

Documentation is another big issue and it is largely regulatory-driven, Knight told us. "There are so many little boxes to check, spread out all over the medical record, and we worry about losing the critical-thinking component, that observation of patients. We've struggled to make the documentation piece very efficient so that a caregiver has the time and motivation for critical thinking and patient reassessment."

To that end, Methodist Hospital recently piloted what it calls "quality rounds," an innovation that combines process change with new technology. Knight describes it "as a dedicated hour during which every charge nurse or nurse manager partners with someone from leadership or quality control, and often with other team members, physicians, pharmacists, and case managers in tow. They make rounds together, gathering information that is then summarized in a very visual way by a new kind of electronic tool we've created. The tool allows the nurse to see in a single glance whether the key quality and safety procedures have been accurately completed for each patient.

"There are two keys, and the big one is what I call point-of-care information," Knight said, "which lets a nurse focus on the things that need to be addressed at that moment—maybe it will be an advance directive or removing a catheter. The nurse will know at a glance when the catheter and IV's were inserted, when the diet was prescribed, or the patient's pressure ulcer risk. It tells the nurse a lot of different things in a single view that would take at least 30 minutes to determine individually." The pilot has yielded very positive results. One hospital has gone more than six months without a single case of the three most common hospital associated infections (central line bloodstream infections, catheter associated urinary tract infections, ventilator associated pneumonia.)

Technology can't work alone, however. Electronic solutions are powerful, Knight acknowledges, but to succeed they have to be "wrapped within a culture." And that requires people work—winning the support of the hospital workforce, in general, and the physicians, in particular.

Electronic solutions are powerful, Knight acknowledges, but to succeed they have to be "wrapped within a culture."

MANAGING COMPLEXITY

Methodist's four hospitals annually dispense almost 9 million doses of medicine in some 17-step process that begins with the doctor giving the order and ends with the patient receiving the medication. Given that most of the steps are human, Knight aimed to plant a series of safe-practice behaviors in the minds of all those who participate along the way. One such behavior dictates that there be no multitasking at high-risk moments, some of which Knight defined for the doctors and nurses while also urging them to hone in on their specific tasks and the critical moments of the day when they needed to be totally focused on patient procedures.

Next, the hospital's clinicians had to agree on how the order sets—that is, collections of predefined orders covering accepted treatments for various conditions—were to be prepared for computerization. To date, around 50 sets have been developed, reviewed, and built. By the time the project is complete, it is estimated that some 400 sets will have been developed. The order sets help to assure that nothing a patient with a particular condition needs is forgotten. They also allow reminders about safety measures, such as prophyllaxis against blood clots. However, each of these order sets had to conform to the computer system's structure and be easy to modify to adjust to the needs of individual patients. Writing each order set so that it would work with the computer system was no easy task; it took weeks, if not months, depending on the complexity.

"You have to find out how any given written order is entered, transmitted, and executed now [before computerization]," Knight says. "The electronics are going to change that process. So you basically do a walk-through from the moment a pill is a fantasy in the doctor's mind to the time it's delivered to the patient. What are all the different steps, and which ones are going to have to be reengineered, and where are the negative side effects we're going to have to fix?"

Fortunately, most medical people are eager to help. "The good part about health care," Knight points out, "is that we have a workforce that, for the most part, has chosen to do good, not just to do well financially. There is an inherent desire to give patients better care, and that helps in getting cooperation because you are going to have to engage everyone in the changeover. You've got to find a way so that everybody feels they're contributing."

A CPOE system is designed to simplify the so-called five rights that are required before medications are administered: right patient, right medication, right route, right dose, and right time. The system is intended to reduce the chance of human error, but it introduces another level of risk, computer error.

Your staff's willing cooperation in shepherding a changeover will go a long way toward easing the inevitable tension that arises when any new technology is introduced and ancient processes are redesigned. But tensions will flare if the new technology itself misfires.

To minimize that risk, Methodist often relies on "Failure Mode and Effects Analysis," a procedure that spots existing or potential problems early on. The analysis uncovered significant shortcomings along the way, notably in terms of how difficult it was for clinicians to operate the CPOE system. For instance, researchers found that reordering a medication required 31 steps, yet when a doctor reordered a previously discontinued drug, the system failed to acknowledge it as an active order. The team analyzed the process and identified 29 problems, which led them to create a new and shorter 23-step prototype that resolved the reorder issue.

The doctors cheered, and once the overall system was free of bugs, they were pleased with the results. They had to be reminded, though, not to place unqualified trust in CPOE, because automation can lead to mistakes. For example, when a doctor keys in a prescription outside the system's embedded parameters, an alert flashes on the doctor's screen. If the sensitivity is set to high, the alert can appear when nothing of any consequence is wrong and the clinical decision is totally appropriate.

Aside from the annoyance, false alerts give rise to a dangerous condition known as "alert fatigue." Doctors and nurses begin to ignore the warning light because it's so often not relevant—then comes the day when it's important, and disaster strikes.

Still, there's a tendency to rely too much on the new technology. Clinicians sometimes let down their guard, assuming the computer will warn them if there's something wrong. Or they see a bar code on the packaging of a medication and assume that it has been adequately checked. Automation can geometrically multiply the effect of a mistake.

DEVELOPING A CULTURE OF SAFETY

"Computer or no computer, administering medication is always a high-risk moment," Knight says. "Computers programmed with flawed processes make mistakes with incredible speed and incredible reliability. You can never completely rely on them." Part of his mission is to incorporate that message into the clinician's behavior. He delivers the message in four key lessons designed to create a truly safe culture:

▶ Keep eyes wide open. You should be constantly observing your environment with an eye to potential safety hazards.

▶ Talk to me. You should be communicating vertically and horizontally—over-communicating, if necessary—with your colleagues and aides so that everyone knows what others are doing and thinking about patient safety.

▶ Stay in the moment. You should be focusing intently on what you are doing, particularly during high-risk tasks. Avoid distractions.

▶ Never abandon your wing men. Always support your clinical team, because the success of medical interventions requires precise teamwork.

As Knight points out, the four rules are counter-intuitive, diametrically opposed to the way we live our lives for the most part. "We multi-task instead of focusing," he says. "We're terrible at communicating both vertically and horizontally. We become numb to our environment. And we tend not to play well with others."

In one of the hospitals, they have chosen to translate these four principles into action in a unique way. Each manager appoints a safety coach in each department of the hospital, whether clinical or nonclinical. Chosen from frontline employees, the coaches work with supervisors to find and address safety risks. Some can be resolved on the frontline; others are more systemic. Methodist has monthly meetings of coaches and supervisors to share their findings.

The meetings also address the chronic problem of an excess of processes. The intricate safeguards put in place to protect against error can tie a system in knots, forcing both doctors and nurses to spend hours in front of monitors clicking through procedures rather than caring for their patients. The application of a little common sense can often break through the barriers without creating new risks.

Most advances, though, result from interviews with individual physicians and staff, asking such questions as: What barriers do you confront? How are you working around them? What safety-related issues keep you up at night? "If you want to know how to do the job better," Knight says, "ask the guy doing the job. That goes for safety as much as anything else."

Most advances, though, result from interviews with individual physicians and staff, asking such questions as: What barriers do you confront? How are you working around them? What safety-related issues keep you up at night?

The new medication ordering process was just one of the many complex tasks Tom Knight confronted, and will continue to confront, in reengineering Methodist's systems. Indeed, from his perspective, as a longtime leader in providing safe, quality medical care, Knight is convinced that the reengineering of U.S. health care delivery will never be finished. He sees health care transformation continuing as long as there are doctors and patients.

The important thing for Knight—and for everyone reading this book—is to know how to recognize the opportunities for reengineering and how to set about making the right changes in technology, people, and processes. That's what we'll discuss in the next chapter.

CHAPTER 7

THE HUNT FOR REENGINEERING OPPORTUNITIES

By now you know that the delivery of health care
can be transformed for the benefit of patients,
physicians, and the people paying the bills. Almost
every area of health care offers opportunities
for improvement, and no area is free of error,
inefficiency, or escalating costs. Clinician after
clinician has bemoaned care failures only to describe
inspirational success stories that address the
systemic causes of the breakdowns.

So where should a clinician, hospital, payer,
integrated health care system, or physicians'
practice begin to tackle its own challenges? As with
all reengineering efforts, targeting specific areas
of opportunity is both an art and a science. Where
you begin will, in part, determine your long-term
success.

CHOOSING A STARTING POINT

The field of work you need to reengineer first might
be as narrow as a single process—say, how an X-ray
gets from a radiologist's office to the examination
room of an orthopedic surgeon. Or, it might be
as broad as the work of an entire hospital unit—
pathology, for example. An even more ambitious

choice—which we wouldn't recommend for a first effort—would be to reengineer the work required in treating a chronic condition, such as diabetes or hypertension, cutting across multiple segments of a health care delivery organization and even going outside its walls.

Even more strongly, we don't advise trying to reengineer a whole health care organization all at once. It's been done, but to do it right literally takes years. Meanwhile, the people involved are likely to retire or change jobs, methodologies and technologies improve, and new complications arise.

Our research shows that several factors come into play in choosing a field of work for reengineering. Most often, a physician sees an opportunity to improve the quality of delivery, outcomes, or service to patients. Doctors often complain about dysfunction, but, in fact, it is dysfunction that points to the need—a.k.a. opportunity—for improvement. Medical error is the most common indicator of dysfunction, but we also saw examples in the form of lengthy delays before diagnosis and treatment, poor outcomes after treatment, a recurring illness or condition that could have been prevented, and initial mistreatment of a patient's problem.

In some cases, the dysfunction was so severe as to put the standing and reputation of the hospital, system, or practice at risk. In other cases, the operating costs of the work involved were so out of control that they threatened the overall financial soundness of the organization. Finally, there's always an element of pragmatism in deciding where to reengineer. Ask yourself: Will the organizational conditions allow the change effort to succeed?

Let's get specific about how to look for reengineering opportunities. To begin:

▶ *Focus on areas of risk.*

The delivery of health care is an implicitly risky proposition, with hazards that extend well beyond the success of a particular medical treatment. Handoffs and complexity make the problem worse. In the previous chapter, Tom Knight amusingly described the sources of those risks, and the challenge of eliminating them when he conjured up the image of a 747 engine strapped to a Kitty Hawk biplane.

"There has never been a run-up in technology like there has been in health care over the last two to three decades . . . other than probably the computer industry," Knight told us. "But the advances have all been in the diagnostic and therapeutic area." We are operating with an outdated delivery infrastructure, and a culture little changed from when Knight finished his residency a couple of decades ago.

It's not a lack of skill among the caregivers that is causing most of our quality problems, Knight goes on. Rather, they're largely due to system failure. It's the breakdowns in communications and repetitive human tasks that are compromising good and reliable basic care, he says. Musing over Methodist's 9 million annual medication administrations, each requiring accuracy in approximately 17 separate steps of delivery, he worries about the potential to do harm. "If you have only a .01 percent error rate, that's a lot of errors."

How, then, Knight asks, do we redirect our complete reliance away from health care providers' knowledge and skills? And, we would add: How do we also get costs under control while we are improving the quality of care?

There's no single or simple answer. Health care delivery depends on a complex set of processes. To help assure that the correct medication gets to the right patient, for instance, technology and processes—robotics, electronic ordering, bar coding, and the like—have been introduced into health care. But the work still consists of multiple tasks with lots of opportunity for error. In many cases, reengineering will simplify the work to be done; in others, increased vigilance and more thorough checking will be needed.

We asked Knight how to spot potential trouble areas before an error occurs. He gave us some sound, practical advice: "One of the best ways to spot potential error is to get the frontline employees together and say, 'Hey, what do you have to work around, what's getting in your way, what's bothering you, what's keeping you up at night from a safety standpoint?'" The potential for detecting errors before they happen and making corrections on the front end is tremendous, he says. You can get incredible information by asking questions and also by encouraging people to report near misses as well as actual errors. Use the error reports, Knight suggests, to figure out which have systemic implications.

In fact, nothing makes the case for reengineering more starkly than facing up to the sometimes brutal truth about performance.

In fact, nothing makes the case for reengineering more starkly than facing up to the sometimes brutal truth about performance. This is not always as easy task. Knight often quotes one of his partners and friends from Forsyth Medical Group in Winston-Salem, North Carolina, Dr. Jack Thomas: "When you have a great reputation, you sure hate to mess that up with data." As with the extraordinary security measures the airlines have been forced to adopt in the post-9/11 world, you will locate the breakdown spots, actual and potential, when you consciously seek out embarrassing and troubling errors. Your next move, of course, will be to begin fixing the processes and behaviors that are contributing to the breakdowns.

▶ Focus on high-cost areas.

There are as many reasons for high health care costs as there are health care experts. Some say the cause is so-called defensive medicine, meaning the sometimes unnecessary tests and treatments ordered by doctors fearful of overly litigious malpractice attorneys. Other observers criticize health care providers who are too focused on the volume of their work and what they bill, rather than on outcomes and value delivered. Experts with an economics bent contend there is not enough competition to keep costs down. Still others blame a lack of evidenced-based medicine for the inefficiencies of the health care delivery system. Then, of course, a growing number of consumers demand the latest pill, medical device, or procedure regardless of whether it offers any advantage over less-expensive, established treatments—and their physicians comply.

Having seen data that supports just about every argument, we aren't comfortable pointing a finger at anyone. But we are positive that high costs limit access to health care. And our experience tells us that areas of relatively high costs in any delivery system often signal inefficiencies, rework, and breakdowns that make them ripe for reengineering.

However, high costs alone aren't necessarily a red flag. We are also seeing extraordinary advances in medical treatments and diagnoses, and such advances invariably raise costs in the early stages of their development. It's in everyone's best interests to pay attention to costs and, at a minimum, slow their rate of increase. Yet, considering the rate of scientific and technological advancement, patients are going to continue to demand access to new treatments. Health care costs will, therefore, continue to rise unless delivery becomes substantially more efficient and effective to offset the costs of new treatments.

We did hear a contrary view from a forward-looking expert who argues that science is advancing at such a rate that replaceable body parts will soon be available, drastically reducing the cost of health care. Got a bad heart or kidney? Just pop in a new one.

Have an injured hand? Just screw on another one. We don't buy his argument, at least not in our lifetime. Near- and medium-term advances in science will only drive up the cost of health care.

Consider what's happened to the treatment for an irregular heartbeat. An implantable defibrillator that costs $25,000 or more has replaced medicine once dispensed by a pharmacist behind a counter at your local drugstore. And an obese person who would have been advised to diet can now choose bariatric surgery, or even a pacemaker-like device implanted in the stomach to send nerve impulses telling the brain the stomach is full. There are some exceptions to the rule, but, in general, innovation will continue to drive up costs.

So how do we lower the costs of health care while increasing the quality of outcomes and access to care? The answer is simple, the execution challenging. Every health care delivery unit, from individual physicians to nationwide hospital systems, must ask whether high-cost areas can be reengineered to lower costs while improving quality. The practice of disease management, where patient care is actively monitored and managed, has already shown that costs can be reduced while quality improves. Better yet, there are still more cost and quality benefits to be achieved.

Cheryl Pegus, a cardiologist with training in epidemiology and biostatistics, told us about the cost-control opportunities in disease management. Pegus currently works as the chief medical officer and head of strategy at SymCare Personal Health Solutions, a venture-capital initiative of Johnson & Johnson. SymCare lets patients submit health and treatment information to a central data warehouse accessed via cell phones or over the Web directly. Physicians and nurse case managers—the latter working mostly in disease management or for insurance companies—can access the data to provide patients with faster electronic feedback from their clinicians. Besides helping patients achieve better self-care, the data can be aggregated to measure the effect of disease management on outcomes.

Pegus points out that five diseases—diabetes, heart disease, hypertension, pulmonary disease, and asthma—account for a large part of health care costs. Most health professionals agree that by focusing on these diseases, delivery costs could be reduced while improving outcomes.

Pegus, however, adds that the process of disease management itself must be improved. It's an area overdue for reengineering. Better information on the relationship between treatment and outcomes is needed, and physicians must be directly engaged in care management. A nurse making an occasional cold call to a patient is not care management. Processes must also be developed to handle patients with multiple diseases, an extremely high-cost area.

Pegus is an optimist, as are we. She believes that both the quality and cost of pharmaceuticals, devices, and treatments are relatively good. And also like us, she believes that the "big area to focus on is the process flow of how health care happens." Excess costs are hiding in health care delivery.

▶ *Focus on the work of the physician.*

Technological, economic, social, and political forces are changing the work of medical practitioners. But it is critical that doctors not allow themselves to be overwhelmed. They must take back their rightful role in the redesign of health care delivery, especially in any discussion of health care reform. On the national front, we believe physicians have been too quiet in the debate over how the delivery of health care must change.

Physicians are at the center of diagnosis and treatment, yet they are increasingly burdened by outmoded delivery systems. They experience all the symptoms of poorly designed work, including:

Breakdowns in information flow. Item: we have heard repeated complaints about the lack of information that referring physicians receive about their hospitalized patients.

Redundant information demands and rework. Item: multiple record systems require multiple forms and reports.

Complexity. Item: there has been little standardization of processes in health care delivery.

Overwork. Item: poorly designed systems are demanding more of physicians, extending their workday without improving the quality of outcomes.

By examining the actual work a physician performs—and how it interacts with the work of other health care deliverers—you will discover how the doctors' lives can be improved while also improving the quality of patient care. Most of the successful examples we encountered were in physician partnerships and practices. Indeed, some of the best ideas for lessening the physician's burden are likely to come from nurses, technicians, and other caregivers who have a close-up view of a doctor's day-to-day life.

Now broaden your focus to include the work that is (or could be) done by these same non-physician providers—nurses, nurse practitioners, medical assistants, and technicians. Think about the specific work that various team members can do. Assess their skills and where they fit into the process, and use that assessment to differentiate their work assignments. You could also take a page from other industries by allowing these caregivers to come up with changes to improve the physician's work.

Southwest Airlines, for example, famously improved its turnaround time by letting its baggage handlers figure out faster ways of loading and unloading. They, after all, were the ones who saw where the bottlenecks were out on the tarmac. The same holds true in medical work. Taking advantage of team members' unique perspectives is a smart thing to do.

Our research has turned up many examples of reengineering that involve the entire care team more efficiently and effectively. As a result, the physicians' time and skills are being leveraged in more productive ways.

▶ *Focus on the patient.*

A main precept of reengineering dictates that change should be made with the customer front and center, and when it comes to health care, the patient is the customer. The mystery is why patients aren't demanding better care. Were it not for the great respect physicians still command, angry health care consumers might already be marching outside hospitals and doctor's offices—and for good reason.

None of us would consider using a bank that didn't provide ATMs and online-banking services, yet the vast majority of us are denied ready access to our own critical medical information. We can get a text message the moment a package is delivered to our doorstep, yet we have to wait one to two weeks for our physician's office to tell us our lab results. We can make or change dinner reservations online at any time, yet we can only reach our physician's scheduler between 9:00 A.M. and noon on Mondays, Wednesdays, and Thursdays, while paying penalties for missed appointments.

Greater convenience is something we take for granted in our everyday lives, enabled through new smartphone apps, online services, and other advances. In some locales, even parking meters can be paid for via text message. Amazing, isn't it, that we don't expect (or demand) convenience from health care providers? Ultimately, health care will change—it has to. Consumers already live in a future that medical providers are just now striving to join. Innovators needn't look far for good examples of how they might improve patient services.

Perhaps the greater challenge is to help patients deal with the fragmentation of health care. These days, patients are challenged by the system. Some are overwhelmed by the process of just getting into it, while others find it hard to navigate once they're in. "We've created a specialist for every part of our body," says Debra Geihsler, a health care executive who has helped reengineer three major delivery systems. "You can't find a general surgeon anymore. You can't find a general orthopedist anymore. You find a shoulder specialist or an ankle specialist. We've parceled out the patient in every way possible." Having sliced the patient into multiple parts, trying to get a complete picture becomes a major challenge. "Which is why," Geihsler says, "in my current work, we are focusing on training our primary-care physicians to have a holistic view of the patient and manage his or her total care."

Geihsler believes that one of the leverage points in reengineering health care delivery is how physicians engage with their patients, especially in challenging economic times when people pay less attention to their own care and well-being. We told you how

she was instrumental in launching an experimental
program in Chicago that placed physicians in the
workplace, centered on patient needs.

In describing the patient challenge and the program,
Geihsler said that "every time there was an economic
crunch, I would see how it affected our patients and
my physicians. Patients would delay their treatment
or not come to see the physician at all, because
they did not want to pay the co-pay (if they had
insurance). They went to the ER if they needed care.

"I tried to come up with a way to reach out to our
patients," she continued, "not just sit back and be
reactionary. We needed to move out into the market
and make ourselves known and get our physicians
busy."

A lot can be learned by focusing on a patient's health
care history. Every case will be different, but all
will turn on the patient's economic condition and
access to care. What will not vary is the importance
of understanding that most patients' health care
experiences can be significantly improved if
physicians and other care managers will simply put
themselves in a patient's shoes, seeing the system
through another's eyes.

▶ *Focus on areas where you can succeed.*

Pragmatism should always play a part in deciding where to reengineer, and the fields of work to target are those with the best "case for action." These areas provide visible opportunity for significant performance improvement, the so-called burning platform. A burning platform might be a field of work where quality problems threaten the safety of patients, or where cost issues block access to needed care. A strong case for action comes from the field that best energizes the people who must execute the change.

Sometimes, though, very good organizations can be blind to opportunity and their own deficiencies. In health care, large research and teaching hospitals can fall victim to their own success. The great medical results they produce make it difficult to argue for even more improvements in quality, patient service, and costs. So finding a place to start process change can be difficult in smart, successful, and polite organizations.

We suggest that you search out areas where teams of people have an appetite for change and great ambition for improving the quality of care. You will know them by their enthusiasm for what's possible, their talk of better patient outcomes, their desire to help patients navigate the flow of care, and their wish to improve clinicians' lives at the same time. They will have great respect for the culture of health care workers but will not fear disturbing the status quo.

Look for areas where there is a clinician leader who can shepherd the clinical staff through the reengineering journey. We've heard it said many times that clinicians can only be led by other clinicians, and even though it sounds like a parochial view, we agree. Reengineering of professional work can only be done by people who intimately know the work, yet are open to change.

TAKING THE WORK IN HAND

Once you have chosen your starting point—whether it's a high-risk field of work, an opportunity to cut costs, the work of the physician, unmet patient needs, or simply the field that seems likeliest to welcome change—the next step in reengineering must be to tackle processes. But since you have to understand processes and how they interact if you are to change them, you will have to draw up a chart of all the processes in your organization.

Your mapping work will take longer than you think, but when you are done, you will understand where time, resources, and money are being spent, and where breakdowns are occurring.

Process maps typically cross organizational boundaries. For example, if your objective is to reduce the time it takes to get radiology results back to the physician who ordered them, you will see processes that start in the physician's office where the order was initiated, processes that instruct the patient, processes that occur in the radiology lab, and then the processes that finally get the results into the ordering physician's hands. Your process map should have a level of detail that shows all these activities and tasks.

Deciding on the actions required to improve performance is both an art and science, and these decisions inevitably begin to invoke the third major reengineering pillar, changes involving people. Here are some questions that might help determine where to begin your redesign.

- ▶ Which processes will need to be changed to accommodate the new technology you plan to incorporate within the next year?

- ▶ Are there activities and tasks now being done by several people that can be combined into the work of one person?

▶ Are the steps in your various processes being performed in a natural order?

▶ Are you trying to force multiple conditions into a single process, or should you have multiple processes to accommodate different conditions?

▶ Is the work being performed where it makes the most sense?

▶ Is the work designed to minimize reconciliations?

▶ Can checks and controls be reduced, or are more checks and controls required to improve quality and assure safety?

▶ Have you provided single points of contact for both patients and physicians?

▶ Is information technology enhancing the work or slowing it?

▶ Is there data redundancy or rekeying of information?

▶ Is rework required, and if so, why?

These questions should help generate ideas about how to improve the work, but still you will just be starting to reengineer your system. To accomplish your objectives, you must continue to manage technology, process, and people as we have prescribed.

One final piece of advice: The quality of your ambition will be critical to your success. The goal of reengineering health care delivery should be a quantum leap in performance, not just incremental improvements. Set aggressive objectives. What's needed are enormous reductions in costs and drastic improvements in quality and safety. Small improvements will not solve the challenges of health care delivery. The objective is to create what we all dream of, and that is, the best health care system possible. What patients and caregivers alike want and deserve is not out of our reach.

One final piece of advice: The quality of your ambition will be critical to your success.

EPILOGUE

Health care reform emerged as a key issue during the 2008 presidential campaign. Following President Obama's inauguration, the debate was particularly divisive both between and within political parties. Legislation gained and lost momentum, and what finally emerged was largely health insurance reform (in contrast to delivery reform), expanding coverage, revising regulations, establishing insurance exchanges, and setting mandates for businesses and individuals.

A number of smaller pilot projects, focused on the coordination of care and quality, did survive. But the work of "reforming" health care delivery is still ahead. In the months and years to come, we expect to see cuts in Medicare and Medicaid, largely driven by the need to fund expanding coverage. These changes in reimbursements will leave no option but to reengineer health care delivery. We see no other way for reducing costs or improving safety.

As the changes called for in current and future legislation are phased in over the next few years, the need for reengineering will become even greater. Hospitals and providers will be confronting dramatic changes in how they do business and engage with patients and providers. Public reporting, transparency, care coordination, outcomes-based reimbursement and other initiatives will put tremendous pressure on organizations to adapt. Those that are experienced with the reengineering process and have the right leadership and methodology in place will thrive. Others will struggle.

The good news is that much of the task of reengineering can be done within the health care system itself. But what is absolutely necessary is the involvement of everyone who depends on professional health care for their well-being, both the caregivers and those who receive their care. All of us must lend a hand—and we must do it now. We can't afford to wait any longer. Lives are at risk, and unconscionable sums of money are being wasted.

The prime objective of broad health care reform, whether by legislative means or by reengineering, is to improve access to health care for the millions of uninsured, while reining in costs and improving quality. The United States is not alone in its quest for top-notch health care at lower cost. China has embarked on a massive program to expand its capacity to deliver care. Meanwhile, wealthy countries in the Middle East are aggressively implementing electronic health care recordkeeping and Britain is embarked on a country-wide effort to standardize its records. Almost every country has some sort of initiative under way to improve care delivery.

But legislation and government policies cannot, by themselves, accomplish broad health care reform. A critical piece of the equation belongs to insurance companies, which must streamline and standardize their processes to help lower the overall cost of care. We have seen data showing that up to 40 percent of the insurers' operating costs is spent on administrative processes, not the delivery of care. And some hospitals write off up to 30 percent of what they bill because of the complexity of approval and collection procedures.

Payment incentives could be better designed to encourage hospitals and physicians to follow proven protocols. Furthermore, overly litigious lawyers must be called to heel in an effort to reduce the practice of defensive medicine and lower the costs of the malpractice insurance providers are forced to buy.

No single book can address all the issues of health care. And we expect that it will take 10 to 20 years to accomplish all the objectives of broad reform. But we have tried to show that everything hospitals and physicians need to improve the quality of care and reduce costs is already available and at their disposal. There is absolutely no need to wait for governments or insurance companies to act. Governments will legislate, and insurance companies will either clean up their own processes or continue to contribute to inefficiency. But, in the end, only the people working in health care can improve quality while also lowering costs.

THE SUPER-ORDINATE QUALITIES

We have shown in this book how inspired caregivers are doing their jobs and delivering better care to their patients. These hospitals, doctors, nurses, and assistants share super-ordinate qualities that can inspire all of us. We call them "super-ordinate" because, at the highest level, they represent the necessary ingredients for successful change in the health care equation.

Here's what the people who are successfully reengineering health care delivery have in common:

- ▶ An ambition to improve the quality and safety of care in dramatic fashion;

- ▶ A deep respect for the experience of patients;

- ▶ A passion for improving the outcome of treatments;

- ▶ A desire to create a better workplace for clinicians;

► An appetite for change to create better medical practice;

► The clinical leadership required to bring about change;

► The persistence to overcome the inertia of current practices and processes;

► A willingness to acknowledge their own shortcomings or detrimental behaviors.

We are convinced that the deep-seated inclination of physicians and other medical practitioners to do good will enable them to embrace and cultivate these necessary qualities for change within their organizations once they face up to the need. And we are no less sure that meaningful reengineering will be speeded up once its beneficiaries are persuaded to demand better health care as their birthright. We write in large part in the hope of raising patient awareness.

LET'S CREATE A BETTER SYSTEM OF CARE

As the engineer and scientist that we are, we have a natural bent for process and systems. But the hard reality is that what we now call a health care system is no system at all. It's a patchwork of parts, or, from a patient's perspective, a series of isolated silos of care that patients must traverse—hopefully with the right information in hand or attached to their beds. From a clinician's perspective, it's a collection of noncommunicating, disparate parts that he or she tries to make work together, while also dealing with antiquated administrative processes that distract from the real work of care.

But the people and systems you've become acquainted with in this book show what a real system of care should look like. It's patient-centric, educating the patient and offering clear choices. Its physicians and assistants are focused on the patient, not a set of administrative processes. Electronic records are accessible at the point of care and caregivers' choices are made apparent. The care itself is managed across a continuum of providers and places, and the practice of evidence-based medicine and avoidance of complications depends on real knowledge. Protocols determine what the physician does first, though prevention of disease and the ultimate health and well-being of the patient are paramount. The kind of care system that we aspire to will not come from a top-down declaration of change, nor will it come from the heavy hand of government. A real system of care can only come from the bottom up, from thousands of process changes, executed by thousands of caregivers, enabled by a robust technology infrastructure, and spurred on by patients themselves.

Let's begin the change we so desperately want and need.

INDEX

A

Ackerman Institute for the Family, 29
Activate Healthcare, 125, 126
adoption times in process improvements, 103-105
adverse drug events (ADEs), 146-153
Advocate Medical Group, 122
American Society of Health-System Pharmacists (ASHP), 153
Atrius Health, 125
attention to detail (electronic health records example), 82-84

B–C

behavior, changing. *See* people development
Blue Cross/Blue Shield of Massachusetts, 50
Brennan, Michael D., 98
"burning platform," 203
Bush administration, electronic health records initiatives, 89

California Pacific Medical Center (CPMC), 113, 171
Camenga, Cathy, 113, 114, 115
Cardwell, Terri, 151
champions, identifying (electronic health records example), 76-77
Chang, Florence, 64, 68, 70, 75, 78, 83, 87-88
checklists. *See* implementation checklists
Chicago Police Department, 122

Q-R

FT Press

FINANCIAL TIMES

In an increasingly competitive world, it is quality of thinking that gives an edge—an idea that opens new doors, a technique that solves a problem, or an insight that simply helps make sense of it all.

We work with leading authors in the various arenas of business and finance to bring cutting-edge thinking and best-learning practices to a global market.

It is our goal to create world-class print publications and electronic products that give readers knowledge and understanding that can then be applied, whether studying or at work.

To find out more about our business products, you can visit us at www.ftpress.com.